Things We Didn't See Coming

Steven Amsterdam

Harvill Secker
London

Published by Harvill Secker 2010

First published in Australia in 2009 by Sleepers Publishing, Melbourne

2 4 6 8 10 9 7 5 3 1

First published in Great Britain in 2010 by
Harvill Secker
Random House, 20 Vauxhall Bridge Road,
London SW1V 2SA

www.rbooks.co.uk

Addresses for companies within The Random House Group Limited can be found at: www.randomhouse.co.uk/offices.htm

The Random House Group Limited Reg. No. 954009

A CIP catalogue record for this book
is available from the British Library

ISBN 9781846553660

The Random House Group Limited supports The Forest Stewardship Council (FSC), the leading international forest certification organisation. All our titles that are printed on Greenpeace approved FSC certified paper carry the FSC logo. Our paper procurement policy can be found at www.rbooks.co.uk/environment

Mixed Sources
Product group from well-managed
forests and other controlled sources
www.fsc.org Cert no. TT-COC-2139
© 1996 Forest Stewardship Council

Printed and bound in Great Britain by Clays Ltd, St Ives PLC

Things We Didn't See Coming

What We Know Now

For the first time, Dad is letting me help pack the car, but only because it's getting to be kind of an emergency. He says we've each got to pull more than our own weight. Even though we're only going to Grandma and Grandpa's farm, he's packing up the kitchen with pasta, cans of soup, and peanut butter—plus the toolbox and first-aid kit. Carrying a carton past the living room, I see Cate there, trying not to pay attention. "Almost done, Cate," I tell her.

"I'm your mother. Call me by that name," she says.

I say, "Mother."

My job is to bring everything out to the car. We'll load it all up when I'm done. He parked in front of our building and put orange cones down on the road on either side of the car two days ago. None of the neighbors said a word and he asked me not to make a big deal. The closeness makes it easy to keep a lookout on our stuff while I'm running up and down the two flights of steps. No one's on the street when I step outside so I go up for another load.

The Benders on the third floor went away the day before Christmas, but Dad said he wanted to wait until the day of New Year's Eve to maximize preparation. He says this is a special new year and we're taking special measures. He says this year I *have* to stay up until after midnight.

Because he's still inside organizing boxes and Cate is just turning pages and not looking up on purpose when he drags them past her, I decide to stay out of their way. To help out, though, I packed up all the batteries from all my games and my portable radio because Dad says they would be useful.

While it's OK for me to hold the key, I'm not allowed to start the car. I think about turning it in the ignition and then saying that I was just checking the fuel gauge, which is all right. But I might get in trouble because I already know he's been to the gas station to fill up, not to mention we've got two big red jugs of gas in the back of our station wagon. Cate knows I know about it because I asked her. She said to just be patient.

I'm sitting on the car, guarding our stuff and scratching at a chip in the maroon paint between my legs, when Milo from downstairs comes out. He acts like he's running out to get to the store before it closes. Then he sees me and slows down and starts asking questions. This is what he always does and it makes my back go up like a cat. Where are we going? How come we're leaving? What am I going to be doing with my lame grandmother at midnight? (He's twelve and is going to a party with friends.) I answer as quickly as possible, keeping an eye on our stuff, not because I think Milo's going to take it, but because I'm trying to figure out why Dad packed all the kitchen knives. Cate sure doesn't know about that or she wouldn't be keeping so quiet right now.

Milo finally says what he's wanted to say since he saw me in the window and came downstairs and it's this: His father, who works in computers, is going to make 125 grand tonight, because he's going to stop blackouts and everything from happening. Once he tells me this, he hangs around a minute, looking at our suitcases and our car. It makes the stuff look bad somehow. He raises his eyebrows at me and goes back inside. He wasn't going to the store.

I know what a grand is because Milo's always telling me how much his father makes (a lot). My grandmother said not to use the word, because it makes me sound like a little gangster.

Finally, Dad comes out dragging the last thing, the cooler, and he's got a bag of vegetables balanced on top of it.

"We're bringing vegetables to a farm?" I ask.

"Just give me a hand."

He doesn't say much about my arrangement of our stuff on the street, but begins right away loading it. He's got that look that means I shouldn't bother him, but I tell him what Milo told me about the 125 grand. He doesn't look at me but he laughs and asks me where Milo's father is going to be working tonight. I say that I think it's the same place he usually does, in an office downtown. Dad shakes his head and says, "He's a dead man."

Cate steps out into the cool air with her bright blue wheelie bag, which looks funny and small considering what Dad is busy cramming into the trunk. She looks up and down the block to see who's watching. The rest of the street looks normal. I hold up my saggy backpack to show her how little I'm bringing, and then she tells me to get my jacket on. She wheels her bag over to Dad, who's sticking cans of tuna fish around all of our stuff. Cate stares at him like she's watching a dog digging a hole that's way too deep.

She gets really close to him and asks, "You sure you don't want to just stick around and knock over a bank when things get crazy?"

He laughs like he doesn't think it's funny.

"How can you knock over a bank?" I ask.

She smiles and tells me she's counting on me to be the only sane person tonight and possibly into the next century. I ask her again how you can knock over a bank, but she starts helping Dad. I stretch out on the backseat so I can listen to them.

Cate says, "There's no reason to be stressed right now. We're all together. We're doing everything to protect ourselves. We're taking all the precautions you wanted."

He keeps packing.

After they finish and Dad decides I can be trusted with the mini-fridge next to me ("That food is not for tonight, it's for the long haul"), we get on the road just as the sun is starting to go down.

Dad dodges cars quicker than usual as we make our way through streets of dressed-up people, some already drunk. In a few minutes, we swing up onto the expressway. Cate says, "Not much traffic for doomsday."

"Can you please let up on the sarcasm?"

Cate shuts down and nobody says anything for a while.

When we're out of the city, she puts on the radio. Pretty soon, we're on country roads, more than halfway there. On the radio, people in London are getting ready for a wild party. I say that it's great that one night can make people have fun all over the world. She agrees and says to Dad, "London Bridge still seems to be standing. That's a good sign, isn't it?"

This makes Dad quiet and angry. She looks at his face for half a minute, then looks out the window. We zip past farms that are dark and farms with lights on and cars parked all over their driveways.

Dad, talking like she's not there, tells me that the world is large and complicated, with too many parts relying on other parts and they all octopus out. Then he starts talking like he's writing one of his letters to the editor, going into stuff I don't understand but have heard a lot of times before. "Our interdependence is unprecedented in history. It's foolish."

I wish I was on a plane over everything. We'd be flying west, going through all the New Year's Eves, looking down just as they happen. I'd have to stay awake for twenty-four hours of nighttime, but I'd be looking out the little window and watching ripples of fireworks below, each wave going off under us as we fly over it. I start to talk about this, but then decide to save it for Grandma. Dad doesn't think planes are safe tonight either.

Cate puts her hand behind Dad's head to squeeze his neck, which means she wants to help him. "What else can we do for you, babe? We're set if anything goes wrong. If it doesn't, we'll have a quiet night of it with my parents. It's all right now. All right?" She looks at me so I can also tell him that we'll be safe. I nod to mean yes, but don't say anything out loud because I'm not sure if it's what he wants me to say or if it's even true.

"What do you think?" He looks at me through the rearview mirror. We both have green eyes. Sometimes, he says, it's like looking in a mirror.

Just then, we bump into the car ahead of us. Not a big bump, a touch, enough to scare everybody. I'm not wearing a seat belt so I get knocked into the back of Dad's seat and a can of tuna fish shoots over onto my seat. It's nothing serious. Cate reaches her hand back to me and grabs my knee to make sure I'm all right. Once it happens I realize that while I was looking at Dad I also saw the car slowing down in front of us, but it all happened so fast I couldn't even call out for us to stop.

The car we hit pulls onto the gravel and we follow close behind like a kid trailing a teacher to the principal's office. Dad says, "Shit!" and punches the button to turn off the radio.

Cate suddenly lets him have it. "Don't blame the radio. It's because you've been so paranoid and scattered that this happened." Here she's talking about something else. "We'll get through the other side and promise me that you'll be better? Promise me." He doesn't say anything. She sinks back and says to herself, "It would just be so nice if things would work again."

I ask, "What doesn't work, Cate?"

Even madder now, she asks Dad why I'm not calling him by his first name.

So I say his name, "Otis," and that makes him laugh.

Dad says to her, "Can't you just be on my side tonight?"

We wouldn't have hit that car if he hadn't been looking at me, but I keep my mouth shut.

Dad turns off the engine. Finally, a woman gets out of the other car. She's not small, and she's bundled up in a lot of clothes. Our car doesn't look any better than hers, but at least we've got heat.

Cate says, again, to herself, "A woman driving alone on New Year's Eve."

I say, "Maybe she's going to a party."

"No, look at her. She's not going to a party."

The woman rubs her hands along the dent on her bumper, then she looks right at Dad. He looks down at his lap and catches his breath. "I can't believe I did this."

"Don't make it a bigger deal. Just talk to the woman," Cate says. Then she reaches her hand back to hold mine and tells me, "Once we're at Grandma and Grandpa's, it'll be quiet. We can see stars and just watch the fireplace till we fall asleep."

"Till midnight," I correct her. I don't think I mind missing New Year's Eve in the city. We'll get up early because Grandma will wake everyone up by clattering in the kitchen, till we all show up to keep her company. Then she'll whip up pancakes and let me stick the blueberries into the batter once she's poured it onto the pan. Dad will be friendly but kind of quiet until it's time to leave because they're not his parents. Unless, of course, the world does end tonight, in which case he'll be in charge of all of us.

Dad hasn't made a move yet. The woman starts rubbing her head with her hands even though it's not itching, the way Dad does when he's keeping something in or about to explode. She's not going to be patient with him, whatever his excuse. I see him in the front seat, seeing what I see as he watches her. It's like we're looking at the same person with the same eyes. He turns his head right and left, checking out the empty road around us.

"Let's go." Dad starts the car.

"What are you doing?" Cate is yelling.

"There isn't time."

As he pulls off past her, the woman watches us, stunned. She slaps her sides and just stares at the back of our car as we bump up back onto the road.

"Dad, I think she's memorizing our plate."

"I can't believe that you would be such a"—Cate wants to say something worse, but I'm in the car—"jerk to a total stranger. You've done a hit and run."

"What? We did stop. She's OK. She can walk."

Cate is rocking in her seat she's so angry. "I can't believe this. And now you've made us your accomplices."

Cate is done, she's facing forward. "I can't defend this at all."

"Have I asked you to?" Dad just drives on into the dark—still fast, with this weird I'm-not-even-sorry look.

Cate turns her head and says to me, "I don't want you to learn one thing from tonight. Not about how to conduct yourself during times of stress, not about how to respect other people, not about how to manage your own insane worries. I want you to look out the window and watch the trees go by, because that's what I intend to do."

Dad taps the wheel a few times with his fingertips to keep from saying anything.

Grandma is waiting on the patch of grass in front of their house, brushing her hair, which always looks so long when she's holding it straight out. On top of her green dress, which she says has been her favorite for sixty years, she's wearing her gray wool coat. When she sees it's us coming around the curve, she puts the brush in her coat pocket and walks out to the road, waving us in as if Dad wouldn't know how to find the driveway without her.

As the car stops, Grandma rubs her hands together for warmth and because she's getting ready for a hug. Cate busts out of the car like she's running out of oxygen.

Grandma throws her arms around her, squeezes tight and gives me a wink.

I climb out and Grandma grabs me by my ears for a kiss on the forehead and both cheeks. "My bean. It's after eight o'clock. You're lucky it's New Year's or I'd already be snoring.

Do you know how long I've been waiting here, brushing and brushing? Since lunchtime, maybe breakfast. It's a wonder I've still got hair on my head, much less feeling in my fingers." She holds me tight. Then she sees the back of our car. "What in the world did you pack? Did you think I wouldn't have put in food?"

Cate bounces the question to Dad with a wave of her hand and walks toward the front steps, where Grandpa's just come out of the house.

Dad's standing by the side of the car, quiet and not looking for a hug. "It's more than food. Papers and things. Just in case."

"Just in case?" she asks.

"We're prepared," I tell her, proudly.

"For what, exactly?"

"For everything to fall apart from interdependence," I tell her.

"Ooh, that sounds unpleasant. Is that what's in store?"

I think something will happen, but I tell her, "Maybe."

She stretches her arms out to a sky full of stars and breathes deeply, until her breath turns into a loud, unladylike yawn. "There. I guess that's what I think about *maybe*. Are you hungry?"

I nod.

"Good," she says and shoves me in Grandpa's direction, but I stay to watch.

She looks at Dad, who's still standing on the other side of the car. "Are you well?"

"I'm well."

"Will we all be eating dinner together tonight?"

"It's been a bit of a day for us. I'm afraid I'm not on board. But thanks."

This stinks. Dad's not going to apologize. He'll hide out in their room all night and the three of us won't be all together at midnight.

Grandma puts her hands on my shoulders and tells Dad, "Unpack whatever's necessary and come inside before the new year starts and everything breaks into tiny pieces."

Grandpa's telling Grandma, Cate and me how one New Year's Eve they invited people to a party and the night was so cold that not one person showed up. Grandma called all their friends the next day and *forced* them to come by for lunch to eat the enormous ham she'd made. Grandma was so persuasive and so many people came that they ran out of food before two in the afternoon. We've all heard this before—and Grandma lived it—but sitting with them in the living room tonight, eating popcorn and watching the fire, hearing the story again feels good.

The clock on the low bookshelf next to the kitchen doorway is humming loudly and saying there's more than two hours until midnight. It's the same faded blue plastic clock that Grandpa carries with him everywhere. When he takes a nap, he puts it down next to him. When he's working outside, he props it up on the porch. It runs on batteries and he brings it to our house when he comes to visit as if it's the only clock he can trust.

Grandma finishes by saying, "That story, by the way, is a lesson for us all that shows you never know what way New Year's Eve is going to turn out. Come midnight, all we might have is the light from this fire. Then how will we look?"

Grandpa says, "We'll be one hundred percent fine. I bought a box of candles the other day. And heaven knows you won't let us go hungry. Nothing's going to be different in the morning."

"But you don't know everything about computers," I say to him.

This gets a look from everyone. I talked back because I had to, because it's true.

Grandpa sits back in his chair, sticks his thumbs under his arms and smiles. "In fact, I do. More to the point, it doesn't matter."

Serious now, Grandma puts her hands in front of her lips like she's going to pray and says to me, "Why don't you get your father? There's no reason for him not to be with us."

Cate throws her hands up, which means I can do what I want.

I go to their room and it's dark. "Dad?" No.

I go down the hall, looking in all the rooms, but he isn't anywhere. Then, in just my socks, I head out the back door into the yard and along the front of the house. Through the window, I see Cate, Grandma and Grandpa inside, all sitting still, nobody saying anything. It's hard to tell if they're bored or if they're what Grandma calls "quietly content." Dad's not in front of the porch either, which I can't get close to or else the light will go on.

I walk out to the car. The grass has gotten damp and chilled and almost icy from the night air, so it crunches under my feet. The car's half unpacked. I go a little way onto the road in front of the house and look for anything moving in the dark. "Dad?" It's quiet and the cold is starting to reach my toes.

When I come back inside alone, I stand in the hall for a minute to warm up. I look in my parents' room again and turn on the light. It's just their overnight bags on the bed that Grandma's made up perfectly, with a little bouquet of holly on the pillow, as if this is some fancy hotel.

I grab my sweatshirt and put it on, even pull the hood up. I head back to the living room and tell everyone, "He wants to be by himself tonight."

"Fine," Cate says. "He'll be better off. He'd worry us for the rest of the evening. Let him rest."

Grandma doesn't approve. "Nobody's better off by themselves when they're like he is."

Grandpa ends it, with "What is he so worried about? It's always been the end of the world. What did we have this century? World War I, the influenza, the Depression, World War II, concentration camps, the atomic bomb. Now he's scared about a computer glitch? A blackout? Let's go about our business. We'll enjoy our hot chocolate with Baileys. He knows what he's missing and can come in here whenever he likes."

I want the hot chocolate with Baileys. Last year I missed it because I fell asleep on the couch too early. The problem now is I promised Dad I would be with him when it turns twelve o'clock.

We play Scrabble; Grandma wins. Cate doesn't seem to be thinking about Dad. There's a little fight about whether the TV should be turned on and everyone decides it's better not to. They say that we should enjoy where we are and not wish we're in the city. Or maybe they're scared of what they might see happening if all the lights go out (and then the TV would go out too).

We look out at the moon instead. We can see the tops of some fireworks miles away when they pop up in a few places above the forest. I leave the others at the window and head into the kitchen for a glass of milk. When no one's looking, I take the flashlight out from under the sink. The hoodie's big enough so that with one hand in my pocket I can hold the flashlight steady underneath and they won't know.

I come back out to them, yawning a lot and saying I'm sleepy. Grandpa tells me not to chicken out. He asks me if I want to help make the hot chocolate and I tell him I'm just too tired. He shakes his head, but Grandma gives me a hug and tells me, "It's good that you know yourself so well. Go to bed. We'll fix up some more in the morning, angel, after we've had breakfast."

"Thanks."

Cate offers to wake me at midnight. "You've been looking forward to this."

"It's OK."

"You need a tuck in?"

I yawn more and say, "It won't be worth it," which makes everybody laugh.

I pad off to my room, making sure the door to my parents' empty room is closed.

I stash the flashlight in the pocket of my pants, put on my heaviest socks, climb into bed and wait. As expected, Cate comes in. I pretend to be falling asleep while she talks to me.

"Are you not staying up because Dad's full of worries?"

"No."

"Are *you* worried about anything? About tonight?"

"No."

"Would you tell me if you were?" She smiles before I do.

"Never."

She throws up her hands, "I've lost him already. The boy won't talk to his mother." She kisses my nose and turns out the light as she leaves. "Happy New Year."

"See you next year," I tell her.

"See you next year," she says and steps out into the hall-way. She doesn't even slow down when she passes their room. She thinks she's still leaving him alone for driving off after we hit that car. Good.

Cate goes back to the living room to have hot chocolate with her parents. I wonder if sometimes she prefers just being with them and not having Dad and me around. Maybe it's simpler and reminds her of being little again.

I put on flannel pants, boots and the shaggy blue sweater Grandma made me for Christmas. Gloves on, I turn the doorknob without making a click and tiptoe into the hallway, walking away from the light of the living room, toward the back door.

The flashlight makes only an orange glow on the ground, which doesn't help as much as the warmth of keeping my hand in my pocket, so I leave it on the hood of the car.

My eyes adjust to the moonlight as I climb up the rocky path that leads into the forest. Looking back, before the trees swallow up everything, I can see more fireworks now, but they're still scattered and far away, only making little puff sounds. I head along the trail that Grandpa has been walking for years, the one he uses for collecting wood for fire.

I know exactly where Dad is and I know he's waiting for me. When we were hiking last summer we found a place not far from the main trail where three trees had come down. They had stood next to each other, but had each fallen in a different direction, so they made a not-so-big triangle on the ground. Dad wondered if someone had knocked them down like this to make a hiding place, but they all looked like they fell naturally and the triangle was made by chance. We sat inside this natural fort, leaning back against two corners, with our backpacks set in the third, swatting fat August flies with our hands while trying to eat our sandwiches.

I remember saying, "This is probably the safest place in the world."

Dad smiled and agreed. "If anything ever goes wrong, let's say that we'll meet here. Even if we're far away, we'll make our way to this exact spot to find each other."

"Deal."

Walking on the trail tonight, I'm thinking my own thoughts. The first is I have to get to Dad by midnight, which, judging by the number of fireworks going off now, must be getting close. I've been here in the dark before, but never by myself. This makes me move faster too.

The second is about how Dad drove off from that woman. Cate was so mad she didn't even tell Grandma and Grandpa about it. Aside from parking tickets, he's never broken the law. He did it because he was in a hurry to get us out here and he saw that that woman was in as big a rush as us. So now Cate is safe in the house, he's safe in the fort and I'm safe here walking through the woods.

I do feel safe; I'm not scared. It's just blackness from the trees, which somehow all looks purple with the light from the moon. It's like nothing's here besides me—no spiders, no deer. Everything is asleep or hidden or someplace else, not thinking about New Year's Eve at all.

The turnoff is somewhere close. Here.

As I make my way in, the branches seem to snap back easily, or maybe I'm pushing harder because I'm a little bit scared.

If it "all comes down" like Dad says, the spiders and deer will feel this New Year's Eve, that's for sure. Depending on how long it takes to get things fixed, everyone will come out here looking for fresh water, for real food that doesn't come from a truck. People will finally realize that they've been expecting too much from a fragile system. Cate says, "If he wants us to move away to the country he should just say so, not put us through this drama." He says he doesn't want to move, he's just thinking defensively. Which must be what he was doing when he left that woman standing by her car. But I bet she drove away mad. Maybe she's somewhere safe now too, watching fireworks or a fireplace or just still on the side of the road there, watching the same moon as the rest of us.

A light ahead, up the hill.

I can see the biggest of the three trees now, this big black log lying there. The light is coming from inside the triangle, a small gold glow in this big forest full of night, making it look warm like a campsite. I say "Dad" to myself. Then I call it out, but he doesn't hear. I run the last little bit over rocks, calling louder now. When I get to the triangle, I see that there's no answer because he's not there. Our flashlight, the one from the bottom drawer in the kitchen, is sticking up out of the ground and that's all. The batteries are low and the light is flickering.

Now I'm cold. Cate was right, I should have my jacket on. Where would he go? I stand on the biggest log and call, "Dad." A big gust of wind makes me have to shout louder just to hear myself, but I balance myself there and keep yelling. Maybe he's back at the house but left this here in case we need to find it later. I'll try twenty more times, each five seconds apart. Giving myself that counting to do keeps me from being scared that he isn't answering, until the twentieth try.

I have to be brave now. When you're meeting someone at

a place like this, you don't always get there at the same time and someone has to wait for someone else. I crouch down, which keeps me warmer. Maybe he got bored of waiting for me. I've got to think defensively too. I don't want to end up frozen. I call "Dad" twenty more times, with the wind swallowing my voice as soon as it comes out of my mouth.

"Hey! I'm coming!"

It's him, running through the forest toward me.

His shirt is unbuttoned and he's sweating. He's out of breath, but smiling. "Oh my boy, it's good to see my boy." He gives a big grin and rests his hands on my shoulders. "Thank you, thank you, thank you."

"I promised I would come so I did."

He thanks me some more. "I've been running to try and get happy out here on my own, to try and stay warm. All I did was get myself wet. And now you're here with me. Good man. Do they know where you are?"

"Nope."

Normally, he would be sending me back right away so that no one (Cate) would get mad, but now he looks out into the woods. Is he thinking defensively? He stands up on one of the logs and pulls me up with him. He puts his hands right under my arms and lifts me up in front of him like he used to, so my head is as high as his and we can look through the trees and see fireworks. They're all over the place now.

"See that?" he says. "It's just turned midnight."

He puts me down next to him and keeps watching. He's

21

intense about it, like an old-style Indian waiting for a smoke signal.

"Do you see anything weird out there?"

"Nothing unusual. It'll be a few hours before we know what's what. You bet I'd rather be here than anywhere else."

"I have a question. Couldn't we have taken her too? The woman in the car. Grandma and Grandpa like visitors, even on special days. Then you and Cate wouldn't have fought and we'd all be safe and together and we could be warm right now."

Dad smiles at me like I'm too young to understand. He gives me a hug and keeps his arms around me. "Let's get out of the wind." We jump down into the triangle and he pulls out a plastic bag for us to sit on next to each other.

"No, we couldn't have taken her. Trust me. It was better to fight with your mother than do that. We're not fighting anyway. And more than that, the rest of them might be sitting in the dark now. Wouldn't that be funny?"

"No."

"Well, I think it would be."

"The lights will come back on sooner or later, won't they?"

"Eventually. I'm not just concerned about tonight as one event. Do you understand that?"

"Yes."

"This whole thing is symbolic, symbolic of a system that's hopelessly shortsighted, a system that twenty, thirty years ago couldn't imagine a time when we might be starting a new century. That's how limited an animal we are. Do you get it?

A whole species that didn't think to set its clocks the right way. We are arrogant, stupid, we lack humility in the face of centuries and centuries of time before us. What we call knowledge, what you learn in school about fossils and dinosaurs, it's all hunches. What we know now is that we didn't think enough. We know we aren't careful enough and that's about all we know. That's what I'm trying to protect us from."

I say, "OK," because he's getting more upset as he talks.

"What else haven't we been paying attention to? I worry about your life, what's going to happen to you. We can't think our way out of every problem. We're not smart enough."

"Don't worry so much."

This only makes him mad. "What's the right amount of worry? In our time, in your time, there'll be breakdowns that can't be fixed. There will be more diseases that can't be fixed. Water will be as valuable as oil. And you'll be stuck taking care of a fat generation of useless parents."

"I'll take care of you when you get old."

He closes his shirt around his chest, but doesn't button it. He's still talking quickly, like he's trying to get all the words out in one breath.

"You can promise to be as sweet as you want, but picture this: The future is a hospital, packed with sick people, packed with hurt people, people on stretchers in the halls, and suddenly the lights go out, the water shuts off, and you know in your heart that they're never coming back on. That's the future, my friend."

It's just us in the forest, but he's talking louder than he

needs to, about things being worse than he's ever said they would be. I want to be tough for him, so I ask, "How do I get ready for that?"

This stops him and makes him really look at me for the first time in five minutes.

"I'm sorry," he says. He changes. He wraps his arms around me and I can feel the sweat on his body as he pulls me close.

He lowers his voice. "Listen, I'm sorry for everything. I'm sorry. I'm sorry." He doubles over, giving me a bear hug, breathing fast, like he's still running.

The flashlight sticking out of the ground is flickering more now. I wonder if that's the only light that's going to go out tonight. I want to convince him to come back to the house so we don't end up out here in the dark in the cold.

I say what Grandpa likes to say: "Everything will be fine until it's not. Then we can worry." He doesn't seem to hear it. He just keeps rocking, telling me he's sorry and hugging me as tight as he can to hold the world still.

The Theft That Got Me Here

The new pills seem to be helping. Her eyes droop less. Grandpa's not optimistic, but that's not news.

The e-mail finally came saying that the city revoked his driver's license. Complaints, citations, near misses. They e-mailed my mother, not him. Kind of patronizing, I think.

"You'll stay with them and help out this summer while he adjusts." Meaning: *You won't see your delinquent friends for the summer.*

Do the driving for him. Help clean Grandma at least twice a day. (That's always life-affirming.) Make their meals with whatever ingredients I can scare up. As if sheer boredom isn't the quickest road to the alternate economy. How could Cate think there'd be enough food for three here, if she's receiving my—docked, until my stupid case gets through the courts—allotment coupons? "Clearly you're resourceful," she said.

Grandpa scratches his knee all day with a ruler and

Grandma doesn't know where she is. Those activities don't burn a lot of fuel so we're managing with the food.

And it's not like he needs me to drive them around. Like all good old folks, he can get ripped off without leaving the house, ordering water and the basics on the net. Still, it's safer than shopping at the piers. So no one's exactly getting dressed up for a Sunday drive. It's been so dusty, I don't think Grandpa or I even went out to the street yesterday.

This *has* kept me on the good path so far, I'll say that. The neighbors are worse off than we are. (Though I've noticed a few lawbreakers keeping tiny squares of lawn.) This place has nothing left to sell except Grandpa's compulsively wrapped wildlife magazines and even a thug such as I wouldn't do that. They're full of those crazy nature greens you only see on-screen. They look more real in print for some reason, even though the paper's all parched.

We'd be eating peaches if this stupid Barricade weren't on.

It's still early, so I may as well do my push-ups.

Break. You're supposed to take two minutes between sets to let the muscles adjust and relax. I drank all my water already, and the tank's in their bedroom. I'm thirsty and they're half-deaf, so no one minds if I go in there.

If they weren't breathing so loud I'd swear they were dead. They're like spoons, with her back to him, his hand on her shoulder. Does he fall asleep like that or does his hand just find its way there every night? Does she wake with a start, this strange man touching her? If they hadn't had more than fifty good years, my heart would break for him.

While I'm in here: Grandpa's got these ferocious pain managers I've wanted to try.

I take two and tiptoe out.

I get back to the guest room and try to do the rest of my push-ups before the pills enter my bloodstream.

I'm doing my last set and everything slows down. No wonder he shuffles.

So I'm lying there decimated, slowed down to a piss puddle of my former self, when Grandma opens the door and *she's fine.* She's standing on her own, not holding the walls, nothing. She's been off the map for six years and now she's looking at me like a professor. Not speedy and scared, like she was on the last treatment, but simply *there,* her old self. And this isn't me on drugs. It's her on drugs. She's got that omnipotence back: She can see I've been into their stash, but doesn't care; it almost looks like she's having a brief perve over the muscles in my back, and she bends down to give them a feel. She's in that orange track suit of hers, the one she wore every day when she could pick out her clothes, and says, "Get off the floor. I'm worried about Grandpa. This thing with the license. We've got to cheer him up."

Grandpa says she woke up like this and he's not asking questions.

So Rip Van Winkle made us breakfast. She seemed put out

at first that there's so little food in the kitchen, but she just made do, cleaning up our crusty mess as she went. Grandpa sat at the table and beamed because she was in charge again. She wanted to make pancakes so he sent me out with ten dollars, and after just half an hour of wandering around (with a steady dose of that melty feeling in my muscles) I was able to locate some milk and an egg—from one of the Chinese sellers. She made the recipe from memory!

The entire time, she's yammering away about Grandpa's license, the restrictive bullshitness (her word) of the urban government, how they'd be voted from power in a minute and get a good dose of what they'd been prescribing. When she flipped the last pancake and sat down with us—not believing she'd been caught without maple syrup—he held her free hand while she ate. I had forgotten they could be like this and it makes me feel like I'm ten again. So I get emotional about her reappearance. Grandma sees it in my eyes— and Grandpa's basically been wiping his tears away all morning—so she gives me a quick frown and shake of the head. "It'll only encourage him."

I formally retract my earlier comment that my heart doesn't break for him, for how alone he's been. But now she's back.

It's almost noon and all the pancakes and excitement left Grandpa snoring on the couch. I'm next to his feet, looking at pictures of jungles and glaciers. Grandma's slamming around, looking at all of her stuff, griping about how we let her clothes get so stained and why the house doesn't smell clean.

Then she comes out to harass me for sitting in the dark.

"This is ridiculous. It's springtime. Here's what we're going to do: We'll take Grandpa to the country. Pep him up."

"We can't."

"No one's taken away my license yet. What's the difficulty? Does the young master have appointments today?"

"There's a Barricade on."

"Then we'll pass through it. I've packed some things. You need fresher air. You look like a hoodlum. Is my grandson a hoodlum? No. Get yourself together. I'll take care of Grandpa."

If I heard right, we're going for a Sunday drive.

"The streets are looking wretched, but once we leave the city we'll see some signs of life. There should be lilacs by now. Maybe we can give Grandpa a little refresher at the wheel? Would you let me do that for you, darling?"

Grandpa's been quiet all morning, just enjoying the show, but he finally tells her she can't drive out of the city.

"They have these checkpoints. You don't know about these."

"I do. I've had nothing to do for the last six years but listen. Of course I know."

"You understood what I've been saying?"

"Everything, my sweet. My love." She adores him, then turns and looks right into me. "I'll take this occasion to say

29

that being talked about in the third person while being in the room is not pleasant." Suddenly I'm thinking about all the times I dipped into her pills when I thought she was lost in the woods. "Can you not do it again?"

"I won't, I promise. But the checkpoints are serious."

"Angel. Grandpa and I lived out there. We're from there." She glares through me. "It's not your criminal record that's going to hold us back, is it?"

Grandpa takes her hand.

"None of us has the right ID."

She puts his hand back on his lap.

"Let's see if we can't enjoy ourselves, all right? I want to give it one shot. What are they going to do, put us in jail?" We say nothing as she changes lanes, almost causing an accident. "Hey, how do you like my driving?"

After an hour spent dwarfed in a lineup of trucks and big cars, we get to the checkpoint.

"Good afternoon!"

"Good afternoon. Where you going today?"

"We're going to visit our old property, sixteen acres in Keaton. Do you know Keaton? I've been unwell and this is my first day better. I need to see some spring."

"ID?"

"Here's all the paperwork from the land. See? And here are our identity cards. Angel, pass yours up."

"These are urban cards. You're not allowed outside."

Her face became this wince. She wasn't surprised or put off by the rules he was trying to enforce. She was just disappointed with *him*. If Grandpa and I had any lingering doubts about her recovered ability to work over a public official—

"Young man. Mr.—what does that say?—Simkowicz? Do I have it right? Gorgeous. My mother's father was from Kraków. Here's the situation, and I'd like you to forget everything else that's happened and stay with me for a moment. My husband and I lived in Keaton for thirty-seven years. How old are you?" The truck behind us honked right then, but she didn't even flinch. "Forget everything else, just answer me."

"Twenty-five."

"Thank you. We bought the place when we were doing well, when the country—by which I mean the *entire nation*—was doing well. We had had our children and were blessed enough to be able to afford that land. Here, this is how it looked when we bought it and this is how it looked ten years later to show you all the work we did on it. Do you see that little rise before the trees start? You're able to see the hills, all the neighbors across the valley, that little pond, the sky above the rolling hills. Three family weddings happened on that hill, and four civil union ceremonies, which, I suppose, tells you exactly what sort of people we are and why we ended up with urban cards. But these were, *all and equally*, beautiful events. And they are still harmonious partnerships, or that's what they tell an old lady. Where do you live?"

"Urban."

"You seem like a sweet man. My grandson's seventeen and hasn't seen much outside of the city parks lately. And I'm sure you know they're mainly dust." She seemed to drift off here for a second. "I wish we were leaving you all with a better story."

"Miss, thank you. But I can't do anything about the—"

"I started forgetting things, forgetting my entire life. Imagine what that's like. They took me to the University Hospital, a magnificent institution. They put me on an experimental medicine, some synthetic proteins that seem to have worked and—"

"I'm sorry, there's a line of vehicles behind you and my job is to—"

"I'm coming to my point. I was admitted to that hospital because I'd been a teacher. My husband can't go there because he worked for a company that robbed its employees. But I worked for the state, back when the state took care of its own. Like you, I had grand and noble responsibilities to all, but I still had to deal with individuals. I'm sure you know the difficulty. Sometimes those two things can be at cross purposes, say, when one child is a bit behind, maybe keeping the others from moving on. What should you do? Ignore the child? I found that I had no choice in the matter. As soon as I started seeing the class as more important than the student, the children were lost, I was lost. Nothing was grand, nothing was noble. Do you understand what I'm saying?"

"I'll get fired."

"No one will know."

"Central will find out."

"Anything named Central doesn't even know what you

look like. I do, and I'm watching you to see that you make the right decision here."

He waved us through.

The last time I left the city was four years ago and the beltway looks just as grim as I remember. No one's living here, because everybody had to choose, urban or rural, and this place is neither. Dry, decaying suburbs. Nothing of value's left, not even windows. The thugs who took over the distribution of resources occupy the biggest spaces they can find here and make them into offices, but they live in the bigger houses farther out. So there's all those little mansions, all this real estate, empty and worthless—whole houses look gutted, like cars that have been stripped and put up on blocks. Grandpa says, "Plenty ironic, these suburbanites who want life both ways out here end up losing the most."

Grandma says, "Plenty ironic."

No one stops us as Grandma drives faster and farther from the city. Grandpa has one hand on her knee the entire time, like it's keeping him steady. They both have this obvious buzz on, because they've made it through the Barricade. (Mine has worn off.)

Her driving is fine, by the way, zipping along between the big cars and trucks—even for someone who hadn't spent most of the last few years in bed. We're the smallest thing on the road, but it's like no one really seems to notice.

It all goes south after she pulls into the empty lot of an old supermarket to give Grandpa the wheel. She does it so sweetly, so wifely. She gets out, walks around the car to the passenger side and tells him to change seats.

"Drive."

"Do you know what they'll do to me?"

"We've already broken laws. And we've got a real live criminal in the backseat."

"All I took was a laptop."

"That's all they caught you with, angel." She is so completely back it's scary.

Grandpa didn't even seem to know how to argue. "I'm old is all there is. They're not about to let me take another test."

"You're driving for me, not them."

He pauses here, to kiss her on her cracked, sloppily lipsticked lips, her false teeth floating behind her smile.

"I'm glad you're back."

"I never left. I wouldn't. I won't"

"So I've got no options?"

"None. Let's go to Bell's Brook"—her destination all along. Not the old property in Keaton, which we all knew had been sold to a salad processor a year after they moved. Keaton seemed more official, since she had some paperwork on it. Bell's Brook is where they honeymooned back in the sixties, the old hippies.

His jerky exit from the parking lot isn't what screwed us. It's that a big car of kids saw a little car. They'd been hanging out there, on the ball field behind, I guess, and suddenly roar down, announcing themselves by screaming, while Grandpa's adjusting the rearview. They're mainly girls

34

around my age (not bad ones either, but a little rough, even for me). Grandpa has read enough reports of this kind of thing to know now is the time to use the accelerator and remember how to steer. He does and we get back on the road, but with them right behind us, shrieking into some big tin cone that we're godless and worse. I slump down in the back.

They catch up in two seconds and start bombarding us with apples. Grandpa stays steady through the pounding. We roll up the windows to protect ourselves. Sad, because we haven't seen apples in a year and now they're drumming all over us. Unthinkable, that people could keep apples from other people. Grandma leans in close to Grandpa as he squeezes through the traffic, trying to get away.

Naturally other kind country folks see we are being harassed, so they start throwing whatever they have handy too. Bread, carrots, peaches. (They have everything out here, all the orchards, all the factories.) Grandpa maintains, though. Doesn't weave, doesn't give anyone the finger. After ten minutes they all seem to run out of interest or artillery. We get some looks, because the car's covered with garbage now, but we finally calm down.

Then the farmland starts on either side and it's like in *The Wizard of Oz* when Dorothy crosses into Technicolor. Tobacco, lush and irrigated to the greenest green. They'd let us die of thirst inside the city, but they keep this tobacco so bright it practically hurts your eyes.

They must have had rain yesterday, because when the sun finally comes through, the air gets all syrupy. We open the windows and inhale one solid hour of leafy crops, manure and all. We look out at all the food, hungry. Grandma says, "Smells like life. Oh, how I miss my garden." But we know enough by then not to try and pick anything. Driving into Bell's Brook, the car gets some more glances, but no more projectiles.

The town is a living poster—baby blue shutters, white fences and smells of freshly baked everything piping out of each chimney. But we speed through, because whatever hospitality is there, it doesn't extend to us.

Their spot is about two miles outside of town, and Grandma recognizes the lopsided maple tree at the turnoff. She yells "Here!" and Grandpa pulls onto the grass and parks behind a thicket of wild artichokes, dense with purple flowers.

She jumps out, hauls her giant purse full of meds out after her, and straightens her hair and makeup, like she's about to go on TV. She walks around the car and pulls Grandpa out. They putter across this little meadow to what she's calling "our hill" while I wipe the car back to presentability.

The chase shook her up and she holds on to him—or he holds on to her—extra tight as they make their way through milkweed, trying to wave the fluff out of their faces. City folk. As they turn to take the easiest path up the hill, I see that each of their rounded backs—her track jacket, his navy cardigan—is dusted with white seeds.

It hits me that I've never seen them both walk away from me. They took me to the ocean once, when I was little, and we stayed in a shack on the edge of the sand. Every day Grandpa brought me to the water and lifted me over the surf of each wave, like I was a prince. At the market, I'd point to a fish, usually a red one, and Grandma would clean and grill it for dinner. I'd fall asleep playing cards on the couch with them and wake up tucked into my sleeping bag on the floor. At the end of any visit, they were always the last ones waving. Now, with this reunion, or whatever it is, I get to watch them walk away, arms locked, holding each other for support on the uneven ground.

So I open up the picnic Grandma packed and see a dozen of her favorite books. Classics, books she used to read, fibrous books (if that's what she's after). OK, so she's not all back, but I take it to mean her mind is hungry, which is good.

Since I can't exactly walk into a country market and use urban coupons—I'm sure all these places are on barter by now—I decide to see what's on offer at the handsome fake mansion that we passed before we got to their maple tree. The three-car garage is sitting wide open with no cars in sight. All their tools just laying out on shelves, free for the taking. If people have fruit to throw around, I'm sure I won't have to walk far to find an outdoor pantry. What a view these bastards have. Half the valley below them is open field, the hillside across is a grove of fruit trees in flower. Beyond that, a forest. And the quiet, except for a car now and then, is like being underwater.

I walk up the porch, turn the knob, and I'm in.

These farmers stocked up on all the electronics when they could. Movies, music, books. Look at the size of these drives they've got. They won't be bored till the next millennium. Mine, mine, mine and mine.

So I'm heading into the kitchen, thinking it should be a breeze—food's the easiest to steal in a big house like this, because there's a lot of it and, outside of the city, not even the top-dollar items would be locked up—when I hear, "Hey kid! Who're you?"

There's this old man in his underwear sitting at the table with his hands folded. He's got that gone-fishing face I know from Grandma, so I do some quick thinking and say, "Your grandson. Remember?" He grunts and settles back, like I thought he would, and chants "Eric" to himself a few times. I can practically see his heart through his skin, his chest going up and down like a motor (probably can't get the right meds out here; we've got that one over them), but he tries to smile and just looks at me as I pack as much of the refrigerator and pantry as I can (a gallon of maple syrup!) into a giant wheelie suitcase they were thoughtful enough to leave by the pantry.

I push it all back to the car, cram this stuff into the trunk—ditch the suitcase, a shame but there's no room in the car—and pack the smoked sausages, sweet potato pie and oranges (!) into the picnic bag, and head out to find my grandparents on their hill.

They're at the edge of the forest, using a flat rock as a bench. They stop talking when I come up. I unpack the lunch, concocting some nervous story of how I bought it in town, but they attack the food without any questions. Sunlight on their pale wrinkled faces, white hair blowing. They look like very happy ghosts. But they're holding something back. Even though they're eating it, they know it's stolen. I'm the disappointment they're stuck with.

We're situated on the exact right corner of the hill so we don't see anyone nearby and no one can see us. Looking down on an aerial plaid of corn and wheat in endless alternation. Fuel, bread, fuel, bread, fuel, bread. In the distance, a reservoir: enough water. More quiet. I'm thinking that we're all thinking about the first Barricade, when the distribution stopped, and suddenly what was in the kitchen was all we had.

Then I find out what they'd actually been thinking about. Grandpa looks at me, says, "We need you to steal a big car." He says if we do, we can stay overnight, maybe at a nice inn, without worry. He says they've got some money we can spend to enjoy life a little. He says he and Grandma will help me do it.

At first I'm flattered he thinks this pitiful forger, this third-rate burglar, could ever land a big car.

But I *am* a good grandson and I put together a scheme for how we could do it. I don't know how to jump cars, but the open house I just attended makes me think we can find some more unintentional generosity.

As soon as I agree, they dig into the rest of the picnic. Grandma gives the rock a polite wipe with her handkerchief, and suddenly they're standing, and ready to rob. "We'll also have to pick up some water," she tells me, like she's starting a shopping list.

So we spend the afternoon on their first crime spree.

We do the water first, which turns out to be easy, as soon as we figure out that the old cabins and farms—the ones staked out by refugees who never got proper plumbing—all keep tanks. More important, they also keep these forty-liter water containers. Grandma's the first to spot them on some old trailer, but there are kids on it, already giving us deadeye. Grandma's insistence on heisting a couple of these tells me she's thinking about more than just an overnight, or maybe she's just being Grandma. We drive through the next town slowly—asking for trouble, sure, but we're on a mission—to find a clear short path from somebody's yard to a spot where she can keep the car running. We find one, some hippie's house, and don't see anyone around. Grandpa stands watch while I pull a container through the mud and hoist it in.

The poor car drags a little from the new weight, but we get back on a four-lane to leave the scene of the crime, and again we're taking in acre after acre of green. They've never felt the thrill of larceny before and I'm glad I could turn them on to it. The two of them in the front, their faces alert, mouths open, the way cats get when you put them outdoors for the first time. They're ready for more.

The big car. This was trickier because we got caught midway. For their sake, I wish I were a more aggressive thief, but I'm only an opportunistic one, so my whole strategy is to hang out in the parking lot at the barter market waiting for some dumb soul to leave keys in the ignition. We put our car in oversize parking, between two trucks that I figured belonged to vendors who wouldn't be back anytime soon.

Grandma, a little spiteful, wants to check out the tacky items these hicks are stuck trading back and forth to each other. Grandpa and I keep her to the task at hand. We become lot lizards, watching people come and go, acting like we're on our way to doing the same, casually popping up on our toes to check into every driver's window for a glimmer of keys.

After half an hour, they find their way into a red Zeus, one of these family trucks, eight feet high, all leather, with fridge and beds, movie jukebox, etc. Grandpa sees the keys and scrambles in. Grandma tosses her purse onto the seat, jumps in the driver's side, switches the engine on and shouts across the lot to me, "And it's got a full tank!" She waves, all excited—*like she's stealing a car*—gets it started, speeds over a median, and suddenly they're out of the lot and on the road. I run to our car, so I can catch up with them at the next rest stop—with the water and the other booty.

When I get back to it, though, a trucker is shooting through the windshield. I keep a distant watch, casually strolling by, hoping he'll lose interest. He doesn't and I keep hanging around. An audience grows, especially once he gets inside and starts looking at our stuff. The electronics, the water. Someone turns the forty on its side, finds a phone number and tries to call its proper owner.

I change the plot. I'm starting to look for another set of keys in another car, when I see Grandma's and Grandpa's little heads in the Zeus pull back into the lot and start to head over to our car to find me. I run across the lot waving my arms to keep them from approaching, but by the time I get there, Grandpa's climbed down, looking at the people ransacking his car and shaking his head in disgust. Some man-and-his-car thing clicks and suddenly he's calling them every name he knows. I'm hiding next to one of the trucks, trying

41

to get Grandma to see me, which she finally does. She hollers something at Grandpa, he shuts up in an instant, practically flies up into the Zeus, then they screech over to pick me up and we peel out in about one second.

Before we're even starting to breathe again, Grandma goes, "I wonder if any of these people out here actually read. Well, it's good news I have my pocketbook then, isn't it? Though I will miss my books. We'll have to try to *find* some more." She reaches into the backseat to give me a poke. I've created a monster.

One or two confused shots were fired after us, more as warnings, but nothing serious. The crowd was just watching, stunned, I guess, that someone from the city would even park there, that an old man would call anyone a fuckwad. He must have picked it up from me.

Turns out what she'd yelled to him that made him forget about his car was "Your grandson's waiting."

We take turns driving this enormous mansion—I have to admit, it's a turn-on—and gorging on the peaches in the fridge. Our hosts didn't leave us water though, and besides that, it's getting dark. We pull off and look for a proper inn.

Grandpa does the talking and we check in with the story that we're from a small town by the city perimeter that the blonde with the welcoming look at the front desk would totally believe existed. He says he found some cash in an old wallet and decided to take me on a little trip.

We get a pizza delivered to the room. Maybe not the most

Italian thing I ever ate but one of the freshest. My mother keeps some basil on the kitchen ledge, but it never tastes right.

So we're spread out in their big bed and I notice they've each put down their slices. She looks at him, meaningfully, and then, obediently, he looks at me. Grandpa says, "We'd like to part ways tomorrow."

I'm like, "Huh?"

"Grandma's better. There's nothing for us in the city. We'll manage out here. We'll find you another car so you can get back."

"What about your ID?"

"I used to have some contacts in government. We can get absorbed in. We might be able to get reclassified. Seems Grandma brought all our savings in the purse. That should ease things for us till we get organized, get our benefits transferred. We don't care about the politics, we'll have a better life out here."

"Without your family?"

Grandma raises her eyebrows at me. "You've got your own life, don't you? We'll organize visits around the Barricades, sweetheart. You've got to finish college. You are going back to school, aren't you?"

"How are you going to explain the stolen car?"

"Who's going to ask to see my certificate of title? They have no Central here. We'll head west and I'll be fine. They may even let me keep my license. Maybe they'll give me one of those trucks to drive."

"But you're not Christian."

43

"Grandpa and I got by out here for quite a while by just being polite. I can talk the talk if I need to. Look: Jesus, Jesus, Jesus."

Then he breaks out his smile that's been under wraps for years and kisses her for the hundredth time since she woke up.

"Your mother will understand. And so will you. It's not negotiable."

I give up. I ask Grandpa for two of his pain pills. He goes through Grandma's bag and gives them over without a fuss. I say good night.

Steal one car and suddenly you're a professional. I don't see why rural would resettle them. Cute as they are, they're not exactly at peak productivity. They might do all right as petty thieves, till Grandpa runs over someone.

And my mother totally won't understand. This is so going to be my fault.

Now it's morning, almost checkout time, their door's still closed. I head downstairs to hit on the blonde and see if all the girls out here are really virgins as advertised or what.

This chicklet turns out to be extra righteous about Jesus and not much more. The come-fuck-me looks turn out to be some component of rural programming. I'm looking at her and thinking somewhere there are girls who aren't this weak, maybe outside of the towns. Specifically, I'm imagining farm girls who look like her, experimenting with their brothers

44

who look like me, when Grandpa comes down looking like he woke up without a kidney.

He brings me back to their room and stands me in the doorway because he can't look. She's in the bed, staring around, blank as she was the day before yesterday. And the sheet bunched across her waist looks wet. He says, "She woke up like this. I've talked to her all morning, but I can't bring her back." He hides his face from me by pushing his head against the wall.

I help him clean her up. He's sure she had her meds, but we find them in her pocketbook, amid all the other pills, and force down an extra dose, just in case. He's slowed down already, massaging his knee, and I can see he needs a nap. I tell him, "Tomorrow might be better," but he shakes his head. I make him take a shower while I sit with Grandma. Then I'll take one. So we'll all be about as clean as can be expected, considering we're in yesterday's clothes.

I'm holding her thin, unconscious hand. "Grandma? We're going to take you home."

Driving back, I'm up front by myself because he wants to sit in back with her. These seats recline practically to beds.

How to explain this car when we get to the checkpoint? We could just abandon it, walk in (if Grandma's even up to the effort) and catch the bus the Barricade workers use. We could try and get through, then see if we can get fuel allotments and sell them for something they need, like nursing.

I savor the trip, take every scenic road like it's our last. It's certainly theirs. We pass around mountains, almost at the cloud line. Terrifying and tempting, driving along the cliff like this.

They don't even look out the window. She's just lolling her head around, confused, jumping every now and then, like it's one long dream of falling. He's stroking her arm, whispering to her. Is it worse that he had yesterday with her—that he was reminded—or was it a gift? *Gift* is the wrong word, since it was taken away, but isn't it all taken away? A glimpse? Maybe that's what life turns out to be. Curtains open. Curtains close. Ta-da.

I try again, "Maybe tomorrow will be better," and Grandpa smiles at me in the rearview. He pulls his seat up to sitting and leans forward to tell me I drive well, that Grandma's proud of me, that they love me. He gives me a pat, then sits back, pushes the seat down again and puts his hand over hers with a loving smack, as if she can feel it.

I don't see what he's done until we're at the rest stop before the beltway. My throat's gotten tight in a panic that I'll never breathe clean air again, so I slide open their door and ask if he wants to use the facilities or wait till we get home. Their eyes are closed and their breathing is rough. They were holding hands between the seats, but now their arms just hang down. Her purse is open on his lap, and so are three empty bottles of pills. Pain managers, blood thinner and heart medicine. A restful cocktail. She chokes a little, then stops completely. I'm just watching and watching and thinking about who I can even call for help, about what little I remember of CPR, about crying, about how I'd even begin to tell anyone, but I'm just watching.

Another red Zeus drives up and parks next to us, a family inside. The fat father gives me the "hey cousin" wave you give someone who bought the same car you did.

I look back at Grandpa as he stops too, as his other hand drops from his lap and lets go of a thick, rubber-banded wad of hundreds. My inheritance. I wave back at the father as he's handing out sandwiches to his kids in the backseat. They're not even going to get out of the car to eat.

I climb in next to Grandma and Grandpa and close the door. I try to move him, try to have his hand reach across to her wrist, but they're both too limp. I pocket the money.

OK.

Now.

Deep breath.

I come up front, turn on the car. Give the family another smile and a wave as I pull out. Cross the highway, turn us around.

Here's what I'll do. First, find a decent place to bury them, which shouldn't be hard out here, with all this endless land. Maybe bring them back to their hill. Then head west, like they wanted. Then? Keep going, as far as the money takes me.

Dry Land

A rain horse is a horse that's been sensitized to travel in downpours without complaint. It can carry packs and people through rising water at a trot. I've never asked who trains them or how, but I'm grateful. This mare never checks me, as long as she's got her hood and body cover on. She'll step through rotten logs in the forest, cross rushing water down main streets to get where we need to get. She's also absolutely bombproof when it comes to thunder or avoiding the deer when they run, and that you can't teach. She was born sound and knows it. I keep the contact secure but easy. She follows, keeping pace as we slop through what's left of the few paths along the hillsides and through miles of flooded farmland.

The problem is, I was never trained to travel in month-long downpours and I'm tired of the damp. But I've got a lot of autonomy. I'm supposed to cover the low areas, look for the shaky light of candles burning in dark houses and evacuate whoever's still thinking the sky's about to clear. Land Management sends me in to protect them from starvation and flooding. Also, my job is to make sure no one gets hurt when the nearby animals finally get so desperate that they stampede through. One county away I saw some waterlogged cattle trapped by a forest that are probably getting close to busting out. They'll either die or find the strength to cross the highway and come through here. I'm clearing people so the animals can push through the empty suburbs and muddy farms, to find higher ground.

It's the people part of the job that isn't so great. I give them the government warning and the pitiable vouchers for relocation. I give them all the good reasons to abandon their homes. I do the social work. The men all tell me I shouldn't be doing this job, the women are mostly polite. The children look at me like I'm the bogeyman. Some guys who come out on these gigs are full of compassion for the human suffering and want to help the families *come to terms, deal with their loss, adjust.* They stay a night to help pack, they get involved. It's a noble calling, if you see it like that, but all I see is people being washed away by life and I think the respectful thing to do is treat them efficiently, not ask them *how it feels.* I like to go in, say what I've got to say, hand out extra meds against rheumatism and ride on to an empty house to camp for the night. A good third of the time they take it out on me anyway. They curse me, call me everything they'd like to call the rain. They act like they're going to shoot me, but they're just broken, and no one makes good on those threats, at least not against a government employee.

Let's face it: Nobody takes this job for the salary. You're on your own all day long with just the rain for company. When it gets to be too much I make the time pass by conjuring sunny days, warm meals, people being happy to see me. That works all right till it's time for dinner and bed. The real reward is having the pick of abandoned property and then hauling away whatever the horse can carry. There are some nice houses out here and making yourself comfortable in a mansion for a night isn't so bad either, even in the rain. Land Management looks the other way as long as we clear out the stragglers. They keep us on horses to prevent us from carrying away too much of the take. They say it saves on fuel, but the way it is now they've got to provide me as well as my horse with enough meds to stay functional. A jeep would be cheaper and faster.

The government trucks are a few days behind us, harvesting the bigger prizes—basically all the construction material that isn't soaked through. Of course, the farmers in the lowlands don't leave behind much that interests me. Weekend people, their houses high up with the views, do. My haul is better if I scour the high roads and pretend not to notice all those little worried lights in the valley.

So I've been out for a week now, crisscrossing the county, checking off empty properties, avoiding the occupied ones as long as I can. Most people know who I am, understand I'm here for their own good. I haven't had to take my pistol out once. They just go quietly. Usually, if they notice me riding around the area, they pack up and leave before I have to even knock on their door.

It's the end of the day, the rain is pissing down and we're in an even jog across what was once a pasture. The grass or whatever was here before has been stripped by a thousand new rivers coming down from the top of the mountain, but the mare's solid on the ground, zigzagging up to a property that spreads all across a flat near the top. No candlelight visible. I'm thinking I should see about sleeping here, when her bridle suddenly gives. The chin strap and headstall have gotten so rotten they've torn in three places. She comes to a full stop to try to shake it all free. I dismount, figure we'll just walk the rest of the way to the house and I'll fix the straps tonight. Suddenly she bucks. Nothing going on around us besides the rain, only her and me, but she bucks. Next, she looks at me like I'd just beat her for the last hour. Then she shoots off in a heat. I've never had this before, never even heard of it with a rain horse. It happens so fast I don't even think of calling for her to stop. She doesn't look spooked, she looks purposeful. In ten seconds she's disappeared into the woods. She'll keep running in a straight shot till she comes to the ocean or drops. That's the end of her. She's got my food and pills, plus the jewelry and batteries I've picked up along the way. All I've got on me, which is about all I've got period, is my sidebag and my water container, and that's empty. Given the forecast for the next month, that last fact doesn't worry me.

So then it's just the rain and the house on the top of this hill. A huge A-frame with solar sheets on each side, collecting nothing but water now. There's an enormous round room in front of the A, with its own cone roof and bay windows looking out to the valley. Even in the gray afternoon downpour, I can see how endless these views could be if it were sunny. There're the remains of a tennis court. Definitely not built for farmers. Plus, the back door's unlocked. People are so blessedly reliable.

Inside, the place is all fake-rustic, patchwork quilts on the walls everywhere, a family of black skillets hanging over the kitchen counter, and the thousand-dollar appliances you can't use since the grid went down. Nice people, tidy. There'll be a pleasant take here once I get dry. I take a pot outside, hold it up to the sky, and in half a minute it's filled for the night. Now I can take off my gear and search for scraps.

Food? God, I would kill for a three-year-old can of soup. The cupboards are bare, nothing, zip. Summer people, they were probably scared to leave anything because they were afraid of bugs. Now I would be so grateful for the protein.

From the living room, I can only see half a field away before it all blurs out to water. There's no wind, so I just hear the rain crashing and crashing onto the roof like pebbles. I take one of the fancy knives, slice into a cushion and eat a few bits of golden foam, just to have something in my stomach so I can sleep.

"Get off my couch!" I open my eyes to a stick of a woman, standing by my head. She's waving the fancy knife over me. She's wild, all cheekbones, wearing some sort of slept-in party dress and too much makeup. She's standing weirdly, continually shifting to get her bones comfortable, the way people get after a few weeks in this climate without the right drugs for it. I reach for the blade on instinct and she flicks it, cutting my fingers. Now I'm holding my hand to my chest and a thin line of blood's coming up. I calculate that I could still take her, if I needed to.

"See what he's carrying."

Suddenly, a softer version of her, about seventeen, is on me and she also looks like she wandered away from a dance party two weeks ago and has been in the same dress ever since. They've both got that pulled look to their cheeks. Food is a memory here. Again, on stupid instinct, I struggle, which throws the girl off and the mother slashes the air in front of my face and tells me to stay the hell still. Her breath is sour from alcohol. Most of the people out here were proper churchgoers at one time, but most of the churches shut down a while back.

The daughter goes through my pockets and gets my identity card and my pistol, which she throws onto the coffee table, knocking over a glass, which falls to the floor and breaks in two. Mother and daughter don't even regard the glass and I realize it's not their house. The mother walks around me, picks up the gun and puts the knife on the counter.

"Have you got food?"

"No. I'm stuck here, lost my horse. I camped out, I thought this place was empty."

"It's not."

"If we can figure out an easy way for you to return my belongings, I'll happily move on."

"Don't do it, Mom."

"I'm only trying to make this calm for everyone. It's my gun, my last bit of personal property. And honestly, it's no danger because there are no bullets in there. In fact, I'd suggest, if you want to keep tabs on me, you're more convincing with the knife. But do what you like, I'm not here to hurt anybody."

With the daughter watching me (a string bean, also rheumatic, I could toss her across the room), the mother looks into the gun. She confidently picks the knife back up, while putting the gun on the table.

"Where are the bullets?"

"In my pack, which is on my horse, and she deserted me yesterday. I wish I had it, I could give you some meds. Is there cat's claw still growing around here? A tea of that might make you feel better." There's a blank look and enough of a pause for them to get that I'm not trying to kill them. The mother's shaky hand, the daughter looking back and forth at each of us. I say, "OK, now that you woke me up, let's figure out a meal," and everyone calms down now. The knife is lowered.

The mother is Liz, the daughter is Jenna. I ask Liz what she's drunk on and can I have a taste. She's relaxed now that she doesn't have to kill me so she leads the way downstairs through a hall filled with Mexican tapestries that would get me a decent amount if I could figure out how to keep them dry and get them to a city. Liz takes my hand to lead me downstairs to a dank clay basement. I see two mattresses that have been dragged just past the foot of the stairs and covered with quilts.

"Why're you sleeping here? It's got to be the dampest place in the house."

"Listen." She's quiet for a second. "No rain. I don't mind the water anymore, it's the noise it makes that gets me raving."

Funny, the sound's never bothered me much. Always made it seem like the weather and people and all of us were more connected. It's the silence, during the few dry months, that seems much meaner to me.

I can make out a wine cellar half the size of the living room, six racks deep, maybe a hundred and twenty bottles on each rack. This I could make a killing on. There hasn't been a proper season for grapes in years. And me without my horse. Five cases of empty wine bottles are stacked in the corner. I take it in, this mother-daughter team alone with all this booze and no food. If I can get them out to some assistance, maybe I can meet up with one of the other guys to retrieve this stuff. Liz uncorks a half-empty bottle of white, hands it to me and says, a little too loudly, "Sorry, it's not chilled," like it's hilarious.

Jenna stays halfway up the steps watching us.

"It's just me doing the drinking," Liz tells me, keeping an eye on her daughter. "Precious gets her sustenance from rain-water." This makes Jenna give up on us and head back upstairs. "It's for the best that she does. One of us should stay sober." She laughs, rubbing her elbows. "Sad thing is it ought to be me."

The wine is spectacular for all I know, but I'm so happy for any flavor at all that I knock a swig back fast. She takes the bottle and guzzles.

"You know what this bottle could be worth?"

She looks at me like I've asked a stupid question. "I guess it'd be worth something. Money, maybe."

Even in the mustiness of the cellar, I can see that before her hair got this dead look to it, and her skin got these new lines, she had a comfortable life. The dress doesn't look that bad. This surviving thing is a recent development for her.

I suggest a trip outside to find something edible before I get drunk. If I can scare up a meal for all of us, she says she'll let me stay. I point out that it's not her house. She doesn't bother responding. I'll stay as long as it takes to get them out. It's my job.

There's a load of flashy rain gear, so whoever the owners are were definitely here for at least one season of rain. Jenna zips and snaps her mother in until she's just a smear of lipstick breathing heavily into the protective flap of treated nylon.

Then Liz starts belting out "Singin' in the Rain."

As Jenna climbs into her suit, she looks over at her mother and says, "You know what? Let's leave you. You're too high."

"Fantastic!"

Liz relaxes fully against the wall as Jenna directs me with a glance to the front door. Good, I can start suggesting options to her.

Liz calls out as we go, "Don't screw her unless she wants!"

Jenna wastes no time in assuring me—"I don't want." She doesn't seem to get that I'm her only choice, but I suppose that that right there is what's wrong with my way of thinking, as far as she's concerned. Once or twice in these last few years there's been a girl whose mind has come all the way around to seeing things the way I do—that you've got to look out for yourself—I have to admit that it isn't that often and when it has happened we've each been so bent on survival that we both walked away empty-handed.

Outside, we survey the property for remnants of plantings, but water has already stripped the ground brown, with only a few rotten roots visible. We pick through what might have been edible a month ago and then I lead her into the woods. I don't find any cat's claw and it's clear that already makes me a fraud in her book.

She's got to shout to make herself heard over the rain: "It's all right. I've had enough tea. I'll take whatever you find that's edible, but I've got to chew it or I'll go out of my mind."

There's a small grove of ash pines at the edge of what was the lawn and they're pretty good. I tear off a piece of inner bark for her to try. She nibbles it and gives me a minor nod, sourly accepting that this is what she asked for. She snags her party dress on a branch and rips it getting free. Hopeless, she's about to cry.

I turn so I can get into my body belt, where the bullets are, and find a plastic string bag for her to use for collecting. She looks at it and I have to explain that her job is to fill it with bark. She looks like she's about to snarl at me, but then goes to work, pulling strips off in quick tugs. She's no good at this work—any work, I'd bet—and two times I have to show her how to tear off bigger pieces. She doesn't say thank you.

"Has she been lit since you got here?"

"She's a drinker."

"You can't survive with her."

"You're showing me how. I watch what people do. I'm learning and I'll write it down later."

"Good."

"I write it all down, everything that's gone on with the farms too. Families being scattered, friends making enemies just so as to stay alive. I've kept dry paper and each night I write down what happened during the day. I'll write about you tonight, what you taught me but also what you are, making money on other people's losses. People won't take notice of it now, but I'm keeping the pages safe till that time they become ready for the truth. There's no way I'd ever burn my writing or allow it to get wet, regardless of what comes."

She's exactly the kind of romantic that's got no instinct to make it. She's fighting the tree, fighting the rain, fighting me, and her whole purpose in life is to record every indignity. If she hadn't put me down so fast before, I'd tell her how smart she is and then try for a kiss, but if I did it now she'd like it too much (the trying, not the kissing).

I find a forked twig at the end of a decent-size branch. I

break it off and poke into some of the promising-looking holes around stumps that aren't already flooded. Most of the time I pull out a tangled sludge of leaves.

She comes over after three minutes, looking miserable, hunched over the string bag, now half filled with bark. Water is dripping off her as she stands still watching while I twist the stick into something soft. There isn't a lot of room in those holes, so once I've actually speared some sort of being, I'm able to drag it out. I keep a hand ready to grab it if it comes off, and I pull out a wet, squirming, good-size rat, pretty well impaled. I stomp on its neck so it stops moving and tell her to relax. She turns away, gagging. We walk back to the house, me holding the animal out on the end of the stick so the rain can wash it clean, her staying a step ahead so she doesn't have to see.

"You'll be surprised how much you like it."

She starts really talking then, and letting the tears go, though she doesn't think I can see. "When my family used to eat at the table, no matter who had done the cooking, there were always three foods on the plate every night—a meat, a vegetable, a starch. Then one by one they disappeared. We complained a lot about the lack of variety when it went down to two every night. Then there was just one, whatever was left, that's when no one bothered mentioning it. We had to eat all the spinach for a week before it went brown, and then we had only potatoes, because that's all we had saved. Soon it was whatever we could find growing in the wild."

"You'd do better in the higher towns, you know. You could go there, for the winter. There's a lot of nice people, country people too. A few days' walk from here. You just have to pull yourself together to do some work."

She holds out the limp bag of bark as evidence she can work. "We'll get by. Besides, they don't want women her age while they're building. She's forty-six, over the cutoff."

And she's a drunk who'll bring you all the way down with her. "You don't understand. This whole area is getting cleared because of the rain. This area is for wildlife now, not people."

"I guess we'll have something to eat then."

"The other animals might not see it that way."

If Jenna leaves, Liz will wander outside and be dead of exposure within two days, guaranteed. Then I can come back for the wine. It's not a heartless plan, it saves one of them, at least. I continue, "There'll be lots of animals using this land, all of them desperate. They'll come inside."

I see her picturing it, the comfortable weekend house filled with hungry animals.

She stops; she knows what I'm talking about.

"My father walked off," she says. "I can't leave."

"But she's leaving you with every drink," I say, realizing how practiced I've gotten at talking people out of the things they care about.

Jenna stays three steps ahead of me the rest of the way to the house.

Inside, Liz, still in her rain gear, has found her way into another bottle. I'd really like to cut her off from what I'm already thinking of as mine. She's broken a stool into pieces and jammed it into the fireplace, and tucked some bedsheets underneath it as her idea of kindling. When we come in, she's rifling through my sidebag looking for a way to light the sheets. Out on her own and she doesn't even know how to make a fire. Liz giggles as I yank the bag away from her, then she sees the rat and goes quiet.

I tell her, "Find a better starter than those sheets." She falls back onto the couch with a crack of a laugh. I look at Jenna, to underline my earlier point. She gets out of her gear and tries to energize her mother into hunting for paper. When she gets nowhere she asks me to start the fire. She says please.

Liz pipes up, "Let's cut our hair off! I'm serious. Hair burns, it smells like popcorn, and then it's another thing we don't have to keep clean."

Jenna looks down at her mother the way a ship looks down at its anchor. She gets her to try some of the bark, but that effort doesn't go far. Liz spits it out and yells, "I want meat!"

I skin the rat in the kitchen and look around for kindling. The problem with these weekend houses is, aside from old books—and there are none left here—no one keeps any paper lying around. In the back of a closet, though, I find a metal file filled with printed photographs. The file is dry and it's packed tight and that's all I need to know. I stopped studying other people's pictures a long while back. Photo paper doesn't burn well, but it burns.

With the photos crumpled and some sticks from an old deck chair, I start a real fire. Liz watches me the whole time, like I'm there to entertain her. "You're from Land Management, am I right?" I don't say anything. "Says so on the bag. Why're you helping us? Shouldn't you be busy pushing us out the door?" I continue not saying anything, which means yes.

Jenna shoots me a look. I've lost her.

"What's wrong with a little bit of caring?" I ask, putting the meat in a skillet and moving it onto the fire. "Everybody needs to eat." Rats fall apart if you try to fillet them. I find salt and pepper in the kitchen. There's not enough for three here, but I'm counting on the gross-out factor working in my favor.

Jenna pours a big glass of water, which Liz waves away as she leans against her bottle. I take the glass, thank her. Jenna says she'll go look for more paper and Liz calls after her, but probably more for my benefit, "Good girl."

I flip the pan to turn the meat on its side. Liz calls me over to the couch for help getting out of her rain gear. "I love my daughter but she's useless." I pull the top part over Liz's head. She looks OK. She stands and fixes her hair more out of habit than for effect. She tells me, "If I had balls, I'd save myself."

I look at her like she's hallucinating. She holds on to my waist as I loosen her rain pants and pull them down.

"I understand Jenna's young, but, once, a long time ago, I was a nurse. Top that. You know what I'm worth out there? Even with my bones feeling like they do, the authorities would provide every comfort. I'd get fixed up and sent out in a heartbeat to one of the cities or care centers. You know what I'd see? A million dying people with no chance. Not for me. Plus, they'd split the two of us up in a second because . . . Jenna's a pretty girl, but my hope is that the world finds a different use for her than that. Without me she'd end up on one of the youth gangs in a week. So, mister, I *get* that we can't stay here like this. But we're just as defenseless if we walk out into the forest. Couldn't protect ourselves from a rat, let alone any larger mammals. If we stay here and stay drunk, I don't know what comes to us, but at least I don't have to say good-bye to my daughter."

I'm on my knees now, thinking how sweet and twisted their relationship is. I hold the waterproof pants around her feet as she steadies herself on my head to get out of them. Her dress brushes against my face. She gives me a pat on the head, but leaves her fingers in my hair, twirls them against my scalp, like she's dialing one of those old phones. Jenna comes back with a pile of ancient magazines. Liz quickly moves her hand from my head as the fat on the rat starts to sizzle. I stand up in a shot and happily take the magazines, keeping an eye on Liz. I realize her face looks different now, calmer, like she wiped off her makeup when I was kneeling at her feet. She's twice my age.

We eat dinner more or less in silence. I show them how to get the most out of the rat and the bark and the spices in the house. I keep looking at them, each thinking she's giving her life for the other, and I'm trying to figure out the best way to get them out of here. Jenna is giving me dirty looks I don't like and Liz is giving me dirty ones I do.

Every now and then one of the nicer-looking female survivors may have a temporary short circuit in my direction. She'll think that sleeping with me could save her house, might lower the waters somehow. I don't dissemble in that situation, but I don't overemphasize the truth either. You take hospitality where you can. I once had to clear a two-story housing complex and there was this woman in a first-floor apartment who wouldn't go. Everyone else had left and I'd given her the fullest dose of funds for relocation—put the papers in her hands—and still she said she couldn't leave. Said she was waiting for her husband to get back, that he was away working for the state, he wouldn't know where to find her. I told her to write a note, use me as a contact if she got relocated. She sat there with her head in her hands and her elbows on a little mahogany table that three days later would be floating away in water. She said she couldn't. She asked me to stay the night, though, and said she'd see where the water was in the morning and decide then. Thirties, spiritual, with candles and shrines all over the place, cushions instead of chairs. No sign that anyone ever lived there but her. The rain makes people imagine all sorts of things.

I stayed. She did it like she hadn't been with anyone in some time, as did I. When I woke up it was still dark. She was asleep, but grabbing on to me like I was a life preserver. I let her. There've been a lot of times with this job when I've seen people holding on to things that didn't make sense, thinking that if they'd just kept a photo album, their mother's wedding ring, a lucky dollar, that it would keep them safe when the water reached the door. That night, in this woman's apartment filled with crystals and little shrines to nothing, the only foolish thing she had to hold on to was me, the guy who was there to tell her to forget it all. From what I've seen, people usually come to reality and save themselves. Despite all the feelings we think we've got for our loved ones and our attachments, when push comes to shove most people figure out how to travel light. In the morning she let go of me, got dressed and left, without taking any mementos, without leaving messages. With barely a good-bye for me. Just closed the door and got on the bus.

So I'm thinking that once I get Liz and Jenna out, if I make my way back to the main station and explain myself or, better, find my mare, I could be back here in a week. They'd be gone or dead or one of each.

Liz has her own plan and doesn't waste time. After dinner, she says she wants to shower out back under the gutter of the house to get the smell of the animal off her. I should shower too. Doesn't mention Jenna. The last thing I want to do is get wet, but the laster thing I want to do is not get laid. Liz tells Jenna, who's looking sick to her stomach from dinner, to keep watch on the fire. Liz seems almost sober, grabs the driest sheets for us as she marches out the side door. I don't need more encouragement than that. I turn my back, strip down in two breaths and turn again to present myself. She's smiling, which makes me feel better than I've felt in weeks. She has me unzip her and lets the dress drop straight down. I pull on her shivering shoulders, attempt to straighten her. She tries to stop massaging her joints, to hold still for me to look at her. It's not so much that she's appetizing, but she needs me. She looks over my body and tells me I'm not as scrawny as most city boys.

Then she says, "Listen to it. That rain. Isn't it spectacular?" Spectacular now? Fortunately, I'm not in my question-asking mode. We're standing there like Adam and Eve, or Abel and Eve, if you count the age difference, which only makes it sexier tonight. She hands me a slab of soap and walks into the waterfall, pretending to keep a respectful distance from me. She drinks a great load of water and coyly wipes her teeth with her fingers. Rat is stringy. She gargles and spits, with an inviting smile. I get under, yelling from the cold, and then rinse my mouth. We can be under for only two seconds before our bodies have to come together for the warmth. Hers is nice, but it feels kind of soft, deflated, like life's gone from it. Still.

We both start laughing at what's obviously about to happen. Just then about fifty deer run up the hill past us. I hold her tight, like I could possibly protect us if they got scared and rumbled toward us. One after another for about thirty seconds, they leap as best they can off the wet ground. It's one of the few times in this job when I do nothing but watch. We can't really see more than their shapes, like shadow cutouts bounding across the black horizon; the rain is white in front of them. You can feel their weight as they pound across the mud. Then they're gone and I'm not cold anymore because I've got a naked someone in my arms. She's buzzed and I'm buzzed.

"There'll be more coming through," I tell her. "Then Land

66

Management. If you don't have title to this house, they won't be nearly as nice as I'm being about asking you to leave."

She licks my chest. "You *are* being nice. I guess we'll have to move on."

"I can make sure you get to a high town safely. Put in a word that they shouldn't split you up."

"All right," she says, like I convinced her in two sentences. It seems sudden, but so does the fact that we're taking a shower, so I feel only proud that I've helped her to let go. We rub each other to keep warm and get clean, staying under the water longer than we need. Maybe I'm inspirational enough to get them somewhere dry. They'll take a day or two, since we're going on foot, but I could use the company, especially if she stays this friendly. They probably will get split up in the new town—skills are skills—but at least they'll be saved. And then I can come back for the wine and the art on the walls.

We come in and stand by the fire, huddled together in the same sheet. I'm feeling a slight added bonus that Jenna, who's made herself scarce, is losing points over the fact that I'm about to screw her mother. I suggest another hit of wine and Liz takes a small, measured sip. It's not her main interest at the moment, she tells me, letting the sheet fall off her back. She's on me, pushing me into the couch. I am grateful and obedient. I'm learning from every move she makes, from her speed.

She is all action, climbing over me, taking what she wants, entranced by her own exertion. Eventually, though, she lets her guard down, her touches get rounder, the kisses get sweeter, and we settle into a rhythm like we've been doing

67

this for years. There's no room for me to move so I lay back and enjoy it all. When I look up I see that her eyes are shut.

The rain isn't so hard in the morning and I suggest we do a quick forage so we'll have a day's supply with us and won't have to hunt for food as we walk. As we gear up for this, Jenna offers to stay behind and get ready while we find food. By now she understands my mantra about what to take: necessities, yes; valuables, maybe; attachments, no. Liz comes with me. She is eager to learn now and keeps the pace. I show her the pines, but she wants to go farther into the forest. I show her a fern, a mushroom. She makes me taste first, before we collect anything.

So she's carrying the bag and I'm hugging a hickory tree, pulling on a knob of amber sap, saying, "It's a quick source of energy," when suddenly there's a fire in my leg. I fall off the tree and land on my back in a muddy ditch. I look down at a hole in the gear where the bullet tore through the outside of my thigh, then over at her. Liz is holding my gun steady as she backs away from me.

"Stay away from us. Just keep away. Don't come back to the house," I hear, under the sound of the rain, as she pulls back into the woods and disappears.

The gunshot, though I didn't even hear it, started a stampede of animals in the area and the ground around me begins to beat. I pull myself next to the tree's trunk and hope they don't come this way. A few dozen deer, looking for a new place to live. They're thin, confused, darting through the trees. For what seems like a while I sit there watching them go and admiring Liz for what she did, what she thinks she's doing. I wonder what it's going to take to make them give up on each other, turn them into survivors.

One deer gets stopped by a branch and then sets off in another direction. I wonder what these animals were holding on for, before they finally decided to save themselves. I wave at them, try to direct them to higher land, but they're too frantic to even see me.

I hold the hole in my pants open so the rain can wash out the wound. She didn't want to kill me, at least not so she'd know she had. The entry and exit are so close that they connect, in a tall O in my skin. It burns like there's metal in there, but I can see the bullet's gone through. Going to take forever to heal. I tie it all up with my undershirt.

I'm soaked now and the bleeding's still pretty heavy, but I've got to get up if I'm going to make it anywhere and I can't exactly go back to them for help. I hoist myself to half standing against the hickory tree, zip open my body belt and see she left me with half my bullets so I wouldn't feel any missing when I put it back on. This is what I get for lying. I won't look at the wound again until later, because nothing can be done anyway.

The rain's easing up, but I'm moving, I'm moving. There was a light in a house in the valley yesterday, maybe someone's still down that way. Someone who might take pity on a government man, see me for what else I am.

I'm imagining the person who finds me. A real country woman about my age, a Labrador, who forgives this mutt.

What else? Let's give her red hair to her shoulders with freckled skin and sleeves rolled up above her hard-worked forearms. She does what has to be done and keeps a smile through it all, a sincere one. She helps me up onto an old wooden worktable where she's made thousands of meals for her family, cuts opens my pants carefully, just enough so she can see the wound. She's all business, taking care of me. I look around. It's a farmer's kitchen, shelves lined with bottles of pickled vegetables stored for harsh weather (and still not all eaten, even now, because she's planned so well). She'll have the exact right topical to wash me up, some secret her family's used for a hundred years. There'll be a metal bucket full of fresh sunflowers by the sink. Dry towels, a gentle touch, golden light streaming into the room through a fault line in the clouds. And this woman, she's so glad to see me. She's waited patiently through all these months of hunger and rain for me to crawl ashore.

Cake Walk

Margo walked off this morning, as soon as the sun started warming up the ground, leaving me to dig up something else for us to eat. There's a stubby gray-green bush around here with tiny yellow flowers all over it and a peppery aftertaste. You can try a bit of anything new, but you've got to give your stomach a day to let you know if it was a good idea. I'm after a leaf or twig, a lizard even, that might have a hint of sweetness to it. Anything that's not bitter would be a real treat. But it's been too dry or we're too high up. Looks like I'll have to do without dessert until we decide it's safe to go back to the city.

She was out of the tent first, doing her stretches, putting on the faded green hoodie, but doing it with purpose, like she was off to a job interview. We ate in more silence than usual, talked about the blueness of the sky, and then she said she'd be going on a hike. I tried not to say anything, but it came out anyway. "Do you want me to come with you?"

"No," she said. "It's OK." So I stayed behind, calm and understanding.

A lark comes by, lands on the big sage bush at the edge of our camp and gives me the once-over. Usually, I wave him and his germs off, but the sun's going behind clouds and I appreciate the company. I let him watch me work on the water pit. I've got it to a depth where there's enough moisture for us to get what we need, but I'm expanding the hole anyway. Margo says it's pointless to dig for more water than necessary, especially in the hot afternoon sun. I say there's nothing else to do.

As soon as the quarantine was called, we managed to find our way out here. We hiked for a while, up over the border till we got to this dull plateau, and haven't seen anybody for a few weeks.

The lark sings a song and takes off. I stand at the edge of the hole and scan the horizon. Our camp is on a rise under a pair of scrappy cypress trees. We use the area between them like a stage; when we're feeling festive, one of us will stand there to make up a story, or we'll stand there together performing for each other. There's another group of four trees a short walk away, but Margo thought this one was less obvious, even if it's not quite as lush. She's always a few steps ahead of getting caught.

I'm looking at this root I've dug into and trying to figure out which plant it's from, if I've tasted it before or if it's worth cutting off and giving it a try. I raise a shred of it to my nose to give it a sniff when my eye notices this guy stumbling toward me in the distance. I squat and watch. He's wearing a brown overcoat, which could mean he's got chills, which is not good news. I suppose this was inevitable. He's leaning on the bushes as he walks—also not a good sign—and staggering. He's heading for the bunch of trees opposite us—as per Margo's wisdom. I hunch up so I can keep watch. He grabs hold of the biggest tree like it's a long-lost friend, bracing himself on it and sliding down till he's sitting at an odd angle against the trunk. He straightens his legs out, pulls the coat out to his sides. Now he brings his knees up and rests his chin on them. He puts his forehead in his palms. It looks like he's feeling for fever.

Slowly, slowly, I crab walk over to our gear. When Margo walked off, she took the gun, leaving me with the knife. I don't blame her, but there's not a lot I want to do with a knife and an infected individual. I look over at him. He's on all fours, throwing up blood under the tree. Such a pastoral scene, I'd like to paint it—the pale late-afternoon sky, the dried green of the trees, the little man bent over like a dog on the ground beneath it all, and the splash of red at the bottom of the canvas, seeping into the soil. He pushes himself back against the tree and rests.

Even with no breeze, he's probably too close for safety. I reach for a mask and climb up to the second branch of one of our trees so I can maintain my watch and stay out of his sight line and his breeze.

I watch for hours. Every time I think he's dead, he turns or coughs or spits.

The night comes down quietly with a sky full of dark clouds. The leaves are blowing so much and he's holding so still that I have to stare and stare just to make sure he's even there.

When the air dies down, I hear him moaning or crying. He jabbers, some long tirade against a lot of people, including God, and cries some more.

All night long, I'm hating Margo for risking my life like this. As if I could have ordered her to stay put this morning. It was the same when we were in the city. We had taken an apartment high up so we didn't need to fight for turf on a regular basis—the daily climb up to the twentieth floor made it a natural fortress. We had a secure generator, markets nearby for trading whatever we managed to put our hands on and a view of ten other buildings just like ours. We didn't steal within the building—karma, etc.

When she'd go off, I'd ask why she didn't take me along. I could have helped with covering her, carrying more away. She'd say, "I like quiet sometimes." I welcomed her back when she returned. She'd be carrying whatever she'd stolen, plus enough water for a rinse. She'd make me follow her into the bathroom to keep her company while she washed off whatever she'd been into. The conversation would pick up wherever we'd left it—a plan for a future heist, discussion of who was occupying the other floors and their habits, what we would scrounge together for dinner—and it would all be paradise again. She'd stand there scrubbing her hands, casually telling me the version she wanted me to hear of wherever she'd been. "I ran into an old friend and we sat by the water," "I just needed to get out and dance with some freaks," "look what I found through an open window." I pretended it was all right and stopped looking for clues to the contrary.

I never liked leaving that apartment, though. When I did, I never managed much more than picking pockets and stumbling onto the easiest thefts. She says it's because I don't like confrontations. Maybe. I get more ambitious when we're the two of us. She always makes me feel safe (and, being small and female, she provides mighty good cover for illicit activity). I like to think I make her feel the same, but I'm reconciled to the fact that she feels plenty safe on her own. Her past doesn't make trusting her any easier, but it all seems to blank out whenever she's around except that now look where it's got me.

As we built this camp, I did hope that maybe her wanderings would stop. They did, for all of ten days. Then they started, same as before, her coming back a day later with a new array of exciting excuses ("I lost track of time following a creek," "I decided to try to meditate for a night," "I found these wild strawberries and got a little lost") and as happy to see me as ever. Now that we're out here and she doesn't have ex-lovers and dealers waiting for her all over the place, I'm thinking maybe she really does need the quiet sometimes. Weird, figuring out that I didn't quite trust her then, but now it hurts to think what she really wants is solitude. I liked it better when I thought she was after more material comforts.

Now the guy is talking. The wind's muffling it, but he's

talking like there's someone right there with him. I push tighter into the arm of this tree. The bark is rough and just resting on it turns into a kind of torture as it slowly digs into me, but I'll hang on here.

From what I've seen of human behavior, you can't ask a person why they're not giving you what you want and expect a response that's going to make you feel any better. Those kinds of questions are a sneaky way of trying to pull some comfort out of the truth, but no words are really going to do the trick. When I was evacuating people, they knew why I was standing in their doorway, but they'd come up with a thousand questions, all of which were attempts to stall or find some loophole in reality that would mean they could stay in their homes. It never changed the facts.

He's cracking himself up now, like he's gotten to the funny part of the conversation.

If it were just me, I could run off now with whatever I could carry. But it's not, and how would she find me? Besides, he'd notice if I started packing up and, even if I was able to keep him back, he'd stay and claim whatever I left behind and be here when Margo comes back and infect her in a second. So I'm guarding our spot until she decides to wander home.

Staying awake up here is not what's tough, but staying quietly balanced is. I've managed to hook my legs around one branch and my arms around another and it lets me stay reasonably still while being vigilant—watching, breathing softly through my face mask, waiting for him to die.

"Ah, you're up there, are you?" A man's excited voice.

I open my eyes.

Above me, the branches of the tree are visible against the sky, the light is drifting in from the east. It's almost morning. I look down and it's him, just underneath my branch. Looking up has made him dizzy and he's fallen backward at the base of the tree, a mess of coat, arms and legs, and a wrecked, gaunt face. He's smiling at me anyway. Warmly.

"Why're you way the hell up there? Think you're a bird?" He cracks up and blows me a kiss, which makes him laugh some more, and that makes him wheeze, which makes him lean forward and cough, and that makes him spit, which he does, spraying our tent red. I'm not sure if it's intentional or not. I don't say anything. He gets up and wanders around our site, touching everything.

"It's only a head cold, my friend, nothing to get up a tree about." He chuckles as he climbs into our tent, mumbling, "A real mother of a head cold." Inside, I hear him stretching out, coughing, getting comfortable. "*This* is the way to live." He unzips the flap at the top so he can poke his head out and leer at me. "How'd you ever find such a spot?"

"Just did, I guess."

"Take off that mask, I can't hear you. Don't be coy with me, I'm your death warrant! Answer me: How'd you make it so long?"

"I don't know." And I don't take it off.

"You'll have to do better than that. Last Man Standing is quite an honor—and you say, 'I don't know.' "

"You might get through it," I tell him. "They say the mortality rate isn't going to be that high."

"They say, they say, they say. Did *you* get through it yet?"

I shake my head. I've seen enough angry people to know the first order of business is to get the topic off me.

"Do you know how you caught it?"

"Does it matter? If you survive—"

"My chances of doing that might get better if you were able to keep some kind of distance."

"What?"

A favorable breeze is picking up, blowing his breath away. I move the mask enough to repeat my request. He ignores it. "I'm only saying that if you survive this, you're going to have it all."

"Thank you. I appreciate your thoughts."

"No, you've got to listen. You're up there now, but—" He crawls out of the tent, suddenly full of purpose. He blows his nose on his sleeve as he approaches the tree. "Listen." He catches me staring at the red-brown slime and takes a respectful step back. He's speckled with streaks of blood. There's a clotted smear of it going through his hair. "Hear this, I'm on your side. You're a good kid. Don't look it, but you must be a strong kid too. I won't mess you up. That death warrant comment was uncalled-for. Sorry." He bows. "You forgive me, don't you? Look," he says, pointing at the horizon, laughing at the sun coming up behind some rocks.

"It's morning, you've got to have mercy on somebody every morning!"

On a different day, Margo and I would still be in the tent right now, the yellow light burning through, slowly cooking us till we start to move. She's usually awake first, knocking the sheet off us, then repositioning me around her until we're too sweaty to stay asleep. Then I'll unzip the front and back panels and let the morning air through. If she's feeling especially tender, she goes out with the designated cloth and sops up all the heavy dew from the biggest leaves, then comes back and wrings half of it out into my mouth, keeping the rest for herself. *Very mother bird,* she says.

"It's a fucking new day. You stay here another month or two and you'll be right as rain. You will survive, I feel it. Here's what I'd do if I was you: Wait it out a while longer. Get all suited up for microbes—just in case, but I reckon it'll have worked it's way through the population by the end of the year—and you go carefully back toward the waterfront. Should be fine there."

He's pacing as he talks, touching everything, manic. There's something normal about him, though, like he was once a good man, but he doesn't think about me or anyone now. He's so desperate to talk, he doesn't care if the other person's listening or catching plague.

"But bring a real mask, not that cotton thing, because the streets aren't going to smell so fresh. Then it's yours. Everything's up for grabs. You wait long enough, the air will be clearer, but you could miss out on some fine acquisitions. Everyone who's hid and survived will be taking what they can. There'll still be rich folk who've kept themselves safe, but not many. You clear out one of their houses in one of those protected neighborhoods and you can live however you like, with or without the security system. When that gets old, you can take a waterfront view. Can you imagine the shit there'll be?"

I'm quiet, picturing all those silent streets in the better neighborhoods, imagining this guy giving guided tours of precious belongings in abandoned mansions, holding open suitcases while I fill them up with whatever I can.

"What? You look like I crapped on your chest. Don't you think that's a stupendous plan?"

"Thank you. Can you go now?" I point downwind.

"You're not jacked about this? You've got a snazzy prognosis. You've only got to take what's waiting there. Doesn't the term *cake walk* have any meaning for you, kid? You're still healthy. How old are you? Thirty?"

"Twenty-five."

"Well, you've had a tough time. But it's not much of a difference on the last day, I'll tell you that. You've got hopes, though. For you, it's all about the future, what you want, it's all about now. You out here all by your lonesome?"

I nod.

"A young guy, all this time on your own. Ouch, you must be parched for a piece. Hey, I'll give you my address; there's not much left to take I'm sure, but there was some classic porn." He coughs and spits some more. "Don't worry, I'm already a few days gone, so I'm much less infectious. *They say.*"

He's not going to get a rise out of me.

"Don't suppose you'd let me linger here a bit? Aren't you dying for a person to talk to? Or is that me?"

I keep quiet. He looks through our stuff a while longer. I scan the horizon for any sign of Margo.

"You wouldn't want me to expire all alone, would you?" Talking to himself now. "Yeah, yeah, we all die alone. I know."

He empties out our tool bag, picks up the knife and puts it in the pocket of his coat. Then he picks up a metal fork and licks both sides of it.

"Give me this, at least, so I don't go hungry?" He loves to joke.

If Margo was here, we would have put a bullet in him before he'd gotten close to any of our stuff.

"Whatever you want. Take the tent."

He laughs. "Right, cooties. Wouldn't it be simpler if you move on and I stay here? I'm the weak one, after all. You could climb down and not look back, not even inhale. Naturally, if you start feeling feverish tomorrow and want a little company, I'd let you come back. You'd be keen for a little conversation then." He gags on some fluids in his throat that I don't want to think about. "But that's who I am, a barely surviving humanist in an inhuman world."

I don't say anything. He sits on the ground, massaging his legs and leaning back against the tent. I watch the material sink from his weight. He keeps his focus on me, while moving on to rummage through the duffel bag.

He tosses one of Margo's bras. It flies as far as his shoe. "What happened to her? Did you have to bury her yourself?

Ugh. I hate that. But it's probably cleansing, gives the relationship closure."

He's smirking, daring me to tell him some lie.

Something clicks. Watching him paw through our stuff, giving me a hard sell on all these empty houses, it switched something off in me. I make a bargain: If he ever leaves me alone, if he dies, if I make it back to the city—no, even if I don't—I swear I'll never take anything that is not mine again. I am done with stealing. It's the way I've been living as long as I can remember, always on the lookout for every unwatched package and every unlocked door—it all suddenly seems barbaric.

"Or are they yours?" He kicks the bra up, but it doesn't go anywhere, it stays tangled on his foot, which gives him another reason to laugh.

And Margo. She'll come back, I'll jump down before she's even close to the camp and we'll just run. If we slowly make our way back—we can keep going like this without stealing until it's safe—there'll be more opportunities for us than just free stuff. History is giving us another road today. She can go off as much as she needs to, but we're going to be honest people. That's my only deal with her and she'll see it my way. Society needs us to be good and we're as able-bodied as you can get. Look at us, surviving out here, two city kids. We can build things, we're imaginative, we can work with people. We can work. I can't wait to tell her how it's going to be.

Sometimes when she's not here I try to dissolve into this one feeling of missing her and it pushes away everything else—this guy going through our stuff, the virus. It's not uncomfortable missing her, actually, and with him down there leering at me with his glazed glassy eyes and bloody mouth and nose, concentrating on her and our future is the only way to believe this will pass. It's like wanting her to be here makes me forget she's not.

I wake up at the foot of the tree. I'm sore everywhere. Margo is sitting me up, pouring water into my mouth from a canteen. She always comes back. The sky has clouded over so there's no clue what time of day it is. My head rests against her chest. She takes a handful of water and rubs it over my face. I know it's not rainwater, or from the creek. It's from the pit I dug because it tastes like dirt, almost sweet.

"Quenched?"

I manage a nod.

She rewards me with a kiss. "You must have passed out right here. You'll be fine."

I open my mouth as she squirts some more water into it.

She looks as if she's assessing my state of mind for a moment, my worthiness for what she's about to tell me.

I nod. I just want her to keep talking.

"I've got a story for us." She always comes back with something. "So when I was on a walk last month I spied this huge campsite, five tents around a fire pit, endless high-tech equipment, all about half a day away."

My face manages to show surprise.

"I've been back a few times, to observe. There's never been any action, day or night. Then yesterday, I walked in—

don't worry, I wore a mask—and I'm standing there in the middle of all this *stuff,* expecting an ambush or bloody bodies; I've got the gun out, loaded, but there's nothing. Just supplies the wind knocked over. And *nobody is home.* My love, it is a beautiful haul. These were not cheap hippies, these people were well-funded survivalists. They were stocked. A juicy first-aid kit, filled with every relevant drug. And here—" She opens up a container of pickles and feeds me one. Ah, salt.

I sit up on my own now. Every bone hurts, I must have slammed onto the tree roots when I fell. So thirsty, I hold out my hands to stand and Margo pulls me up.

She says, "We'll take what we need from here and go check it out. The location isn't as choice as ours, but I felt safe the moment I walked in there. They all must have wandered off to die at least a month ago."

I shake my head. It, something, doesn't feel normal. "Too sudden" are the first words I manage. My hip hurts, my arm is scraped up from the tree. I look at the tent. It looks bashed in, with dark stains across it.

She keeps talking. "*Honey bear,* I'll put it more gently: I'm sorry I forgot to bring back a floor plan and decorator samples, but would you mind discussing the possibility of relocation to a bigger place?"

I calm down and nod. For some reason it feels like I've given up.

"Good, we like compliance. You'll be happy when you see it."

84

"I see you really missed me." She's looking at her bra, lying in the dust ten feet away. I don't know what she's talking about. She looks at me tenderly, with pity, then takes my head in her hands and tilts it to give my forehead a long kiss. "You know when I'm away that I miss you exactly as much as you miss me? Exactly as much. Exactly. You know that?" I nod. She says this and I feel safe. She nestles into me, takes a lick of the sweat from my neck. "I know those overnights can be lonesome, but, sweetie, I just washed these." She walks over to retrieve her bra from the dirt. As she's bending over to pick it up, everything comes back to me.

"Don't!"

We're crossing the canyon now, in as much of a rush as I can manage, racing the sun toward the horizon. It's dropping behind the cliffs, putting us into shade. We washed with what was left of our antiseptic and then abandoned everything but the two-handled plastic water jug we're carrying between us. I'm fairly sure our visitor didn't touch it, as it was down by the creek. We're hiking quickly, trying to get to the camp-site—and its pharmaceutical stash—before either of us gets any symptoms. We're keeping quiet because there's not much to say until we get there.

It's been a sweltering day, but there isn't vegetation around here to hold on to the heat. The temperature's drop-ping as the winds come around low, people-shaped rock for-mations, which make it look like we're walking into a dead crowd. The sky turns from orange to brick to gray. It's easy to feel chills and fever at this hour, but we march on, keeping those thoughts to ourselves.

I've remembered the deal I made on the branch and I know that even going to an abandoned campsite is immoral. That word never used to have meaning, it used to be what the other side said, but my visitor—we passed his body as we left, he was under one of those bushes with yellow flowers, curled up like a cat, with a small pool of blood coming from his lips—changed me. When he was talking, I kept looking at his little dark teeth, the paste around his mouth, the spit sloshing around in there—it was like a future mirror. Just listening to him tell me what I was going to steal felt like a deal with Satan. I have not, repeat, have not, found religion, but life has presented itself in these stark terms, like they used to use in political campaigns: I feel *fallen*. And what else am I left to think, with the two of us as we are now, lugging our water, fleeing, permanently banished from everywhere.

No, that's not right, we're sun-scorched and dirty. It's never been Eden. I've always been a thief. Meeting Margo didn't help. We were ransacking the same store at the same time. I noticed her when I walked past the back office and she was emptying out a desk. She closed the drawer with one hand, then looked up at me, caught—but not so caught that she didn't mind pocketing a few items with her other hand. The whole scene made me hard. Even though we weren't there together, I felt free enough to ask her, *Is there much here?* Like we were on the same job. She walked past me, jammed a diamond-crusted personal organizer into my hand, flashed her smile up at me and said, *I don't know what you're talking about, you must be seeing things.* It locked us together forever: *Is there much here?*

But we don't have to accept it. It doesn't have to be our journey. No. Now is as good a time as any to change. It's all about now. I am resolved. I am solved.

If we make it through this is too soft a guideline. There's no need to wait for any more signs to be my best self, no need for there to be a bargain. I can start from now, without conditions: We take nothing. I won't even make allowances for the drugs at the campsite, we can walk right past them. If we are going to make it, we can make it without theft. This is not about God, it's about me and the way I want to live and die.

She looks at me. "How's your hip?"

"It's all right. Worn out, though."

"You're doing your quiet thing. Are you sure he never touched you? You can tell me, I won't leave." I never thought she would.

"I don't remember."

"Then talk to me."

I have no idea how to begin with her, to tell her I don't want to go to this place she's so excited about. I still have a headache from dehydration. "Can't you talk?"

She laughs at me. "If you'll pretend to listen. Here's why I think we're going to be better than ever. They said some people were just immune. Maybe we inoculated ourselves when we ate those pigeons that time, before we knew it was in birds."

"Maybe."

"Is maybe good enough?"

"Maybe. Yes." We walk on. "I still don't get it. If you saw this site so long ago, how could you keep it secret?"

"Wanted to make sure we could get access before getting you excited."

"There's nothing else to talk about out here. I couldn't begin to keep anything from you."

"That's for sure." She laughs, swinging the jug low enough to graze the sandy trail.

My need is suddenly and surprisingly high. I want to ask her where she's been every time she's ever left. And then I want to see files, documents and images that support her words. Surely there's a database somewhere that could provide me with proof. The first time she left, she said, *I'll be back. What else matters?* At that moment, nothing else mattered, so I didn't say *Because I want to know.* It didn't seem fair to insist. She's ridden out on that exchange ever since. But it's mattered every time and I need to know details. If we're going forward, I've got to know who she is. Nothing slides from now on.

I sound like a preacher. I can't talk like this to her. If I even say the word *fallen,* she'll drop the jug and run a mile. No, I just want, I just want—

I just want.

I want the jug gone. I want her hand in mine. I want to trust her completely. I want to know we're in this together.

. . .

"There it is." She points to a sunken oasis. It looks like some lake bed that still keeps enough moisture for plant life. Several blue tents—not the government ones, the pale expensive ones with filter systems—are clustered together amid the trees.

It's instinct for me, the desire to go see what's been left, to put a price on every bit of it, to figure out what I can use and what I can haul away, to imagine the people who bought it all and laugh at their futility, to move in and make their world mine. But if we continue walking toward this mirage, if we change our shells even this one more time, I am *sure in my blood* we'll doom ourselves to always live exactly as we have lived, inhabiting whatever corner of the world isn't nailed down, never staying anywhere long enough to make anything real. We will be the ghosts that feed off the edges of life.

"Did you see them?" Margo yanks me down behind a shrub.

"Who?"

"Shh!" We peer up and see the camp is alive with people, moving around, shifting things, taking supplies. She scoots up onto her knees to keep watch. I am relieved: The decision about staying here is made for us. And at the same moment, I am guilty that the decision was not my own. We look at the water container between us, three-quarters empty. It's all we've got.

The bush we've ducked into is big and heart-shaped, like someone clipped it that way, with thick and shiny leaves and bark that's nearly black. I didn't even bring the guidebook (he touched it), but the bush reminds me of something I once tasted in a forest farther north. I pull off a twig and split it. Inside, the fibers separate like the white meat in a chicken breast. Even with the sun going down, there's the faintest glimmer of moisture inside the twig. I press my tongue to it. The flavor is sharp at first, and then blessedly sweet. The syrupy flavor stays here, fills my mouth, feels instantly easy. I finish it in a bite. It is what I've been waiting for and the appearance of this bush here, where we had to stop, is all the proof I need that I am on the right road.

I split another one and hold it up to Margo. She obediently kneels down from her surveillance position. I look at her eyelashes as she presses her tongue against the twig.

Silently, I ask her to marry me. I want it the way people used to do it—in the middle of a garden, in front of family and friends with everyone still alive. A long wooden table filled with roasts and vegetables and cakes. Three nights of dancing and drinking on a hillside.

She gives the twig a nod of approval. "Good work, scout." She sits back, next to me. "Looks like it's what we'll be living on. Should we march in waving the gun and tell them all the stuff is ours?"

"It's not." I yank off a thicker branch and break it in half.

"That's never bothered you before."

"I'm trying to see the positives."

"I'm so sorry about this," she says.

"Don't be. We had to leave that place anyway. Let's move, maybe these people are sick too."

I'm content. I chew on the twig, sucking hard. The sugar

reaches my pulse, like licorice, and I am awake and at ease at the same time.

"They don't look it." Margo idly checks my eyes, my lymph nodes, my forehead; she has me check hers. "Fortunately, neither do you."

"True."

"So what do we do now, my strangely calm lover?"

I stand up slowly, soundlessly. She grabs me by my belt and does the same. The scavengers are lighting a fire and settling in for the night. They don't even look in our direction. We're outside, the invisible ones again. But we're all right. We'll walk until we're a safe distance away and find a few trees we can sleep under and hope it doesn't get too cold.

"We keep moving," I tell her.

"That's all we've ever done."

"It's going to be different now."

She grins at my sudden certainty. "How so?"

"It just is." I don't know if it's the sap from the twig or what, but I've never felt so confident in my life.

Uses for Vinegar

That could only be her. The others are still covered in soot, still wearing the clothes they were in when they ran out of their houses. They've got kids on their shoulders, folders with papers flying out, enormous string bags filled with their valuables, and, always, the government water in the green containers. Right there in the middle of the line. Low-key, traveling-light Margo, waiting patiently. Like a civilian, except her hair's combed, and her face is washed. She had to know I'd be servicing this event.

Just deal with everyone in front of her and think only about the job.

"Name? ... ID? ... Proof?"

Used to be I'd wait for the fires to be out, for the flood-waters to go down or, at minimum, for a reasonable count of the dead before coming near a site. Otherwise Rescue sucks you in: It's two pay grades up but why expose yourself to the trauma? This time, I'd balanced the account after some windstorms and there was nothing else to do, so I came.

These fires, despite the heat, had mostly burned themselves out when I got here, so I set up the tent this morning. Brownlee was clearly never much of a city, and it hasn't been pushed up the Most Livable List with this recent incident (deep-ground oil drilling at the center of town, compromised fault line, no rain in fourteen months, ignition). What didn't burn on its own was encouraged by locals, so the Guards herded everyone into the pop-up barracks under a nasty round-the-clock watch. To add excitement, some Brazilian bug with a one-inch stinger has gotten comfortable since the last dry spell, and the heat has simmered them into mating season so the air is dotted and dangerous. Apparently it feels like lit matches being dropped on you for the first hour and then it calms to just one lit match being held in place against your skin. They like climbing in hair, so Central has us all wearing caps. I'm keeping my attention half on the bugs, half on my clients, and now half on Margo.

Clearly the locals who are still around are only waiting for me. I'm in Verification, I distribute the cash grants that let them start over. It's sick being loved like this.

The couple in front of Margo are drunk, probably since last night, so you can bet the financial picture about to unfold across my counter will keep her waiting a good while.

"Are you applying for a grant?"

It all went so far wrong when I got the commission to disburse the cash grants. This took me up a whole security level, which somehow I cleared. They expected me to stay at the sites until the last survivor had been resettled. Problem was, Margo's work was with immediate referrals for families, so she'd be waiting for me for days after she was done, with too much time to play with.

That's how she met Shane in Rescue. Red hair, blue eyes, stupid and curious. Calmer than me, visibly so. Stronger than me, it goes without saying. He started hanging around our tent (during the Summer of Hurricanes), working his swagger into all that conversation about death tolls and the weather. I'm skinny, awkward and official, and Margo herself is not immediately apparent to people. Except for these tiger eyes of hers, looking at me now, past everyone else. I was glad to think she'd helped us connect to someone easygoing, some-one our age we might see at other sites, someone friendly. When our shifts were all in sync, we ate our meals together. When civilian provisions were stretched, we pooled our allotments. Shane stayed in our tent when he fell asleep once, drunk off some sherry he'd bought from a survivor.

He was waiting when our bus pulled into the next site—floods, I think—standing around like an entry-level helper, unloading equipment, though he'd sworn to us over the pre-viously mentioned sherry that he'd never do that kind of work again. I was suddenly that nervous guy, putting things together, seeing that if I were Margo and shallow, I'd be choosing him too. I reacted, as she would say. I put him down. Then I asked where the rest of his team was. Rescue had moved on, he told me, but he hadn't. He was maybe going to stick around—he said it with a question in it.

Margo looked scared and gave me that sympathetic flicker she'd give her patients when we'd pass them at mealtimes.

The last glance I had of her was after the coastal attacks two years ago. I had just started in Verification, she had finished training to work in Grief, but both of us were helping out Rescue because we were that green. It was on a street of town houses that had these identical miniaturized plantation facades. Unnecessary double staircases curved four steps up, and a tiny useless balcony over the front door was held up by plaster pillars. Most of these had had their back walls blasted off from one of the explosions (it was a domestic incident). Exactly the kind of scene that gives me nightmares now. I wake up with a speeding heart, convinced there's a boy at the end of the cot (me?), in tears, begging to be taken back home, only it's blown up and he doesn't know that yet. I take his hand to lead him there. And then I wake up.

Looking for survivors, I walked into one of these houses. Squatters had clearly been in there for a while. No couch in the living room, no dishes in the cupboard. Filthy plates on mattresses, clothes wherever they landed. And stolen stuff everywhere else. Nice things too, a closet full of camera equipment, a bag of wallets and ID cards. They'd probably been robbing their neighbors for months, waiting for some grand getaway, and were out when the wall of fire came, unless they were barbecued and vaporized on the back patio.

I was about to call Rescue to tell them to seal the place against looters, when I saw her standing in a bedroom. Little Margo, wearing all this tough yellow gear. She was stealing again, like when we met, jamming useless objects into her fire suit. I hadn't clipped anything since conning my way into Verification, but I could still enjoy watching someone else do it, especially her. I turned back to my tasks and pretended she wasn't there.

Eventually I got myself reassigned to the reconstruction of the area and dedicated myself to that. My supervisors knew our past and seemed to know not to mention her. Big job, over two years at a desk, and it only made me scrawnier and more official. I barely know how to sleep anymore. It's miserable work, looking at devastation, and I've had no one.

And here she is, all grinning and expectant.

"Next."

Come to me.

I didn't even see. Shane's been standing with her the whole time. He stays back in the line as she steps forward. Margo braces herself against my counter with both hands.

"Hello, handsome."

"Are you applying for a cash grant?"

"Come on. When can we talk?"

"Are you applying for a cash grant?"

"Please don't make this harder. . . . OK, yes. I'm applying."

"Name . . . Name? Identification?"

"All righty."

She takes out three identity cards and puts them down between us, like a poker player. All of them have her picture and bar code. One lists Brownlee as home. Not one has her right name.

"Why are you showing me these?"

"I wanted to see you."

"I have to report false cards."

Margo glances over to Central's desk. No one's even looking our way.

"Ten to one says you won't."

Shane's squatting, making bubble noises at the kid behind him in line. I feel teased. For being on my side of the counter, for being straight-arrow, for not having stayed and fought for her like some gallant knight.

"Don't worry about Shane," she tells me. "He doesn't let me out of his sight, but he can't hear us." Margo leans over my counter and gives me a friendly leer.

Behind Shane, the rest of the crowd is sprawled out across the compound, all the way to the Grief tents. No matter what she's after, I'm going to be here till after ten tonight.

"Please go," I tell her.

She looks at me like I ruined her birthday plans.

I say, "There are people waiting," loud enough for the people waiting to hear.

She shakes her head and steps away.

Shane gives me this weird smirk as he tries to approach. He holds out an identity card that I don't even look at as I wave him on.

They didn't get stamped, they didn't get grants, they didn't get reported.

Margo comes to me at night, of course.

The camp stinks of vinegar more than usual, because it's a fire site and tins of it are hung around tent poles to keep the burnt smell from upsetting the survivors. And we're washing our hair with it (lice), and washing our fruit in it (contaminants). Plus someone's figured out that if you drink a quarter cup of it a day, the Brazilian stingers seem to leave you alone. And, believe me, none of that comes out nicely at the portable toilets.

I've been sharing a tent with this psych doctor from Grief. He can't go to sleep sober, so by the time he's on his cot he's near coma. Margo probably asked around and knew this, because she makes a loud entrance, over his snores, She unzips the door and enters like a stripper, like she used to sometimes, with the vocal drum roll, and so on. Humor.

I'm lying there in disbelief, paralyzed, under the hemp sheet we used to bring with us everywhere.

"Just take your fraud somewhere else."

"Come on, the cards were only to get your attention. Well, they were part of the plan if my information wasn't correct and I had to deal with an official official, but I didn't come halfway across the country for a grant. I've got a job. It was just to show you I care."

"What?"

"For you, always." She opens her eyes. Her face, her smile,

slips into an apologetic frown. She puts her palms on my cheeks. "My future, your hands."

"I can't—"

"You know you can." She rests her forehead against mine for a moment. "Our chemicals still work."

"The Chemical Basis for Love" was a scientific article I was always threatening to write about us.

"Shane?"

"He thinks you're going to give us a grant. And it's his car. It's not romantically ethical, but I wanted to get here and my resources are limited. I haven't had a raise since you last laid eyes on me."

"I haven't been laid in longer."

"Your own fault, but we can fix that right up."

She gives me a slow burlesque wink.

"You're twisted."

"For you, always."

It's too much to believe. I tell her, "Just go."

Today I processed 127 former residents of Brownlee. Checked out their finances, their lost assets, helped them close out the mortgages on their exploded houses, dispensed 42 grants, and filed for a favor with Relocation to get Margo and Shane bussed out of here without having to see them again. People were being sent up north for farmwork and I got them into the first convoy, which left after supper tonight. It's work they can do if they need work. If they refused, they'd still have to leave the compound. Whichever.

It's almost midnight and no sign of them. I'll circle once more to make sure they're gone, and if I see them I really will tell Central about her cards.

The doctor says I seem edgy and should join him for a drink. Maybe he's right. Everyone else is on some pill for coping. That's how they sit up all night with each other at the folding tables, telling jokes, remembering neighborhood picnics, a life that probably was never even that great. It's like a wake for a town. They exchange whatever contact information they have left and go their thousand separate ways.

And this is exactly the kind of cohort that wants to talk to me about religion, about *what's happening*. Some tattered manic, still in her singed housedress, will insist I sit with her for just one quick second. Then, high on rapture, she'll borrow my pen (forever), pull a scrap of paper from deep in her handbag, which now contains all of her worldly garbage, and sketch out one of those Second Coming timelines with all the pertinent signifiers for judgment day—plagues, storms, floods, fires—never taking her wizard eyes off me. I'll get that slight nausea that tells me: Sure, that's exactly what this is. Jesus will come home and you'll be caught holding a big bag of Eternal Damnation. But I still don't buy it, or maybe tonight I'm just not that enticed by the Kingdom of Heaven.

The crowd's even mangier, now that the willing workers left with the first convoy. Brownlee was integrated under some Diversity Charter, so the faces have that satisfyingly broad palette for dissemination, but the people here know they're all exactly the same. The same because they ran out of

100

luck (money) somewhere else. There isn't even the normal steady din of crying in this camp, except from the few children, because most of the people here are used to this kind of change in plans. Brownlee is the name of an executive; this place was never meant to be anything more than an oil well.

There they are. I knew she wouldn't get on the bus.

They put up their tent, right outside the cordon and naturally Security does nothing. She doesn't see me. Fine. I'll move my pack to one of the emptied barracks. Even if she gets back in, she won't find me. I'll get a clean cot in a corner, somewhere quiet where I can pretend to get some sleep.

The ones who are still here—their paperwork's not settled or they're getting permission to reenter their houses to hunt down grandpa's ruby belt buckle or something—they're laughing about their dumb luck for surviving. But they have this newborn worry in their faces. They may not know it yet: It's permanent. The cash grants are a nice gesture, but meaningless in the long run. The people in Grief work hard to push the line that rebuilding heals all. Margo told me how insidiously they do it—it's practically brainwashing. The thought is nice: *You'll have a clean slate, a world of opportunity, you'll never look back.* But nothing really heals because, if you lose everything once, running becomes part of you and you're always looking back.

Margo can figure out any guard's weak spot, so I'm not surprised this morning when she comes at me as I'm leaving the showers. I'm in the red-and-white-striped towel that distinguishes naked personnel from naked survivors. I haven't done a push-up in years. Everything about me has only gotten worse.

"Stop pretending we have an obstacle here. You've looked at every record that exists on me. You left your name on all the searches so I would see."

"So?" I have no defense.

She reaches for my shoulder. I pull away.

Turns out she was trying to brush off one of the stingers. It stings. I shriek like a girl and immediately break into a sour sweat.

It burns with a slow pulse, as promised. I tough it back to my new tent without the will or the power to keep her from helping. Margo lowers me onto the cot in the corner and goes through my pack for my medical kit. She takes the tweezers and unscrews the curly spike, barely managing to hold me still for this bit of surgery. The heat seems to be spreading down my arms so she runs to find some vinegar, which shouldn't be hard. I'm supposed to be at my counter in fifteen minutes. She returns, dips the corner of my sheet in the vinegar, and as soon as she dabs it on, the pain cools. I sit up. She keeps putting more vinegar on me till it runs down my arm, my stomach, and onto my lap, almost tickling. She sees an in, pulls at my towel.

"Looks like we're going to have to get you back in the shower."

It's too much. My shoulder still throbs, my brain still

throbs. I double over, shaking. She's never seen me do this, but it happens every few months now, usually when I'm alone. It looks bad, I imagine, but it will pass. It feels like it won't.

"I'm scared. I'm scared."

As usual, she knows how to handle me. "Here: Keep your eyes closed, turn your face to the sky. Your head has to be facing up."

She puts both hands around my neck and holds my head up to the dim solar bulb.

"There. Now do this: Imagine for one minute that everything—everything you're afraid of, everything you're worried about—is going to be fine. Imagine that. It's going to be fine. I'll stay till you're calm. There's nothing to worry about. There really isn't."

It's all worked out: I'll verify Shane, give him a cash grant. Take the identities of two of Brownlee's least-missed dead, make up new cards with their codes (she can get them from Medical), approve *them* for cash grants and work up north. Margo and Shane will sell their car and get on the bus to avoid being traced. I'll sign off on my work, as usual, and then disappear, as would be usual, for the standard week or so, until the next event demands my presence. Tonight, I'll get on the same bus as them, as if it's a coincidence. At the Mid-City depot, she'll explain to Shane what she swears he already knows, that it's over. Then she and I will get on a bus heading north. She won't tell me where to. It's a surprise, but it's somewhere we haven't been, a town so small and out of the way it doesn't even have any resettlers there. We'll be invisible.

And what will Margo and I do when we arrive at this new paradise? Use the grants that go with the new identities and start our lives over, like everyone else. Enjoy being the least-missed dead people from Brownlee. Get reacquainted. Wait for the next event to push us along.

Most evacuees don't learn. They try to start over some-place exciting (a target) or temperate (subject to floods, fires or earthquakes). Or they identify this month's most thermo-politically neutral region. They assume they're not going to have to pack again. Even though it may be the third or fourth time for some of them, they're still completely tweaked with relocation fever. Full of piss and, as the expres-sion goes, vinegar. They take their first steps around their new home and get confident; make friends, buy appliances, plant tomatoes. You want to shake them: *Do you really think this time it's going to be different?*

We're on the bus to Mid-City now, part one of the plan. Margo and Shane are in the back, convincingly sleeping on each other. My pack is on my lap. You never let go of your possessions when there are evacuees around.

I'm in front, with the rest of the personnel. Because I've been off this circuit for so long, they're all strangers to me except the psych doctor, who today is completely sober and feels like chatting.

"I'm going to catch up with these cool guys who've been camping up in the southern mountains for years. Predictable weather, enough food to find. I'm collecting some supplies for them, then heading out. Come. They've got all the equipment. You need some air, man, you look like hell."

Fortunately, he's carrying half a bottle of Cuban rum. I've got government-issue mixed juice and it doesn't take too much negotiating to get him started. I engage. I elaborate my difficulties to substantiate his diagnosis. It *is* hell, I tell him, having access to the documented histories of everyone's bad investments, that I never wanted that kind of power, that I haven't spoken to my parents in years, that I spend hours and hours alone, and, finally, that I saw an ex and it hurt.

He knew it was love-related and wants details. He says different despairs play differently on the body. Love trouble comes through the eyes. Material loss shows around the mouth. True bereavement changes the whole posture. He hasn't had one steady relationship since he started with Disaster Services and, if someone would just give him a grant, he wants to study the damage this work does to relationships because he sees it all in his own face too. As if he's going to get a grant for that.

I tell him how pathetic I've been, longing for Margo, making excuses for her, how I blamed myself when she left. The drunker I get, the louder I get, hoping Shane wakes up and hears me, and then maybe I'll get to fight for the love of my fair maiden. I absolve her. I canonize her. I tell the doctor

105

about the chemical basis. He laughs at that one, puts his arm around me, practically force-feeds me another swig of our cocktail.

"If this doesn't work, try a cup of vinegar. That'll fix your pH."

At the preordained stop, I climb over him and push through the crowds, into the station, running for the bathroom and a toilet to throw up in. It's a full purge, not merely everything I've ingested over the last twelve hours, but every face I've had to help since I started. Every collapsed life I've had to walk into and convert into dollars.

There's a crowd of haggard men waiting for showers, but somehow I look so rough that they push me up to the front. I'm grateful, but don't want to see any of them again or hear about how unprepared they were for their tragedies. I just want to shower.

The water sobers me up. I only ever signed up for the money. If I hadn't taken a government job I would have gone completely under. Still, I've wanted out of this one since the first day. I strip off my clothes, already rancid and our journey's just begun. The thought that Margo's back and she's the one showing me the way makes me get on all fours and heave again, this time with tears, directly over the drain. I stay like that, the shower on my back, the temperature never stable, scalding, then ice, the water swirling the floor clean under me.

From behind the stall door, a voice tells me my time's up.

The clean towel provided is rank, so I dry off with my shirt, perfuming myself with my sweat, which Margo used to huff happily. Pheromonal purpose, she said. I put the shirt back on and catch myself in the chipped mirror, a scared boy of thirty, a man, dressing for an ill-advised date. *You look like hell.*

I am now off the map. The doctor will wonder for a little while what bus I got on, but that's about it.

Margo is out there slipping away from Shane. Do I care? Does she? Is there anything gained by even explaining why you're leaving? Talk does nothing; she knows that better than anyone.

Outside, I head for the northern bus depot. I have nothing to show. She said she'd get the tickets. She's got our new cards. If the driver decided to trigger a search, I'd be in far more trouble for holding fraudulent ID than she would.

A peppy family in matching overalls is in front of me, going on about all the work they'll do when they get to wherever they're going next, like they're talking themselves into it. The father will teach the son carpentry. The mother will get a job in records at a hospital. They seem fairly confident. They've got three old suitcases and an enormous thermos of water. The mother's carrying an old paper bag filled with small spotty apples and carrots for the long ride, and that's all.

I ask them to hold my place while I look for Margo. At the other side of the station, the eastern bus pulls out. There's a lull as the terminal sits, bustles, waiting for the northern bus to come through the night to take us away.

I get back to the line and keep waiting.

The idea sinks in: I am a sucker.

I never saw the cards once she got the new codes put on. She might have changed the names; then I'll never find them, not even to report them. If it's true, if she really tracked me down to get the cash grants and to forge new ID for the two of them, if it's true that I *helped them* into their new lives, I'll just go back to work like it never happened.

No, she has enough clearance and enough craft to forge the grants and IDs without involving me. She would have had to *want* to leave me standing at a bus stop. There'd be no gain. Unless she wants me to stop looking at her records. Maybe all my searches haven't made her feel touched, just violated. I've tracked her everywhere, giving her a little electronic tap whenever I felt sorry for myself. I would have done it forever. No, this makes no sense. She could have just had me blocked.

There has to be a reason for this to be happening. There's a lesson here. There's got to be a reason.

I'm scared.

I sit on the ground and inhale deeply, imagine the history of the world collapsed into a minute, the sum total of every halfway *I love you* ever spoken, all spilled out into the air. I look at the murky reddish moon (sulfur from the fires). I close my eyes and keep my face up.

"How are you doing there?"

I open my eyes at the spotty apple, the mother's hand, her fleshy arm, my future.

"Have one. Eating calms my mind when I get frantic."

"No, thank you. I'm fine." Extra-convincing when you're hugging yourself and rocking.

Try and focus on *what is:* A station at the center of the country. Money, a job waiting. That's more than everyone else here has going for them. And all that mother-loving freedom. I could get on the next bus straight east and see what shape the coast is in. I could camp out with those survivalists. I could track down my actual mother-loving mother, see what trouble she's gotten into and with whom. Or Dad, Jesus.

No. They've been predicting a heavy storm season, so I may as well be back east for when work kicks up again. I drag my pack over to buy the ticket to Durham.

I stand there, scratching my shoulder, my sting.

Her voice: "What are you doing? I've got our tickets already."

I turn.

"I thought you weren't coming."

"Why wouldn't I?"

She pulls me away from the crowd, locks her arms around me and we finally finally kiss.

Her pack is on both shoulders, her bedroll and her jug of water hanging off it. My equipment is at my feet. A dozen times we would have died, but Margo saved us. She knows all the nuts and berries. And how to find your way by the stars. And the value of everything. She's just given Shane the bad news and I don't care. It feels like it used to. She's a real survivor.

She lets go, tells me, "We've got to hurry if we're going to make it." The mantra for the rest of our lives.

She slips my new identity card into my shirt pocket. Her

hand stays on my chest and she leans in closer. She rests her forehead against mine and tells me to close my eyes. I obey.

"I'm not even going to say sorry because you know me. You know how I feel and I know how you feel. We'll fix it."

When she speaks, her mouth is right in front of mine and it almost feels like I'm saying the words with her. *We'll fix it,* like there's something I have to fix too.

I nod. I'm granted another kiss.

She smiles, like something amazing is about to happen.

"Enough sentimental, let's get out of here," she says and pulls us toward the bus.

The Forest for the Trees

I'm on the terrace of the main campus, in a recliner doing my work, the screen propped on my lap, my shirt off. The wisteria is blooming like crazy as a last gasp against this sun. I can see for miles. Margo and I are nearing the end of our second practical union, so I'm taking a break from rewording a speech on male infertility to retrieve the renewal forms. The government changes the wording every six months, so you've got to be sure you're current.

They've made it simpler. You check the boxes, declare intent to proceed as responsible—though not necessarily monogamous—partners for eighteen months, with an option—if mutually agreeable, of course—to renew. Each party is assured of companionship, as well as care, if care is needed, for the designated period. If the contract is not renewed and care *is* needed, the state will provide (pitifully, of course, but that's life).

The practical part: If she were to run off now, I feel assured that she would come back. It's almost like marriage, except it doesn't crumble at every whiff of infidelity.

Behind me, Juliet announces herself by the sound of her sandals on the wooden boards of the deck. With a subtle nudge of my finger, I close the practical union window and go back to working on her masculinity initiative. Her body is solid like an athlete's, and the boards creak a little wherever she pauses to admire the treetop view. The sound of her uneven steps, ambling across the terrace toward me in a semi-purposeful line, indicates she is probably high.

Still, she manages to sneak up behind me and stick her fingers in my ears. She's always nearer than you think, reading over your shoulder.

"That clause makes no sense."

She's also usually less high than you think.

"I'm still writing it."

"Ooh, tone," she warns me, as she rests her hands on my shoulders, leaning down to allow a kiss. I turn my head up so her plum-colored hair tickles my face. For a moment it feels like a position of worship and I'm being blessed. She smells like caramel. I push my mouth against her neck and give a light friendly lick. With her thumbs on my neck, she gently turns my head back down toward the screen. "When are you going to finish my speech?"

Truth to tell, I was only half interested, but I like her to think I'm always ready. "Soon."

"Good. And soon for you too," she says, bending down to taste the sweat on my shoulder. I catch her head there with my hand and press our necks together, which feels so comfortable, even in this heat.

I could easily move up to three-quarters interested. I suggest a shower.

"Later. With Margo. She's never as salty as you."

"I'm sitting in the sun."

"Even so, it's strong or just too manly. I'll let you work. I should head into the city for the afternoon."

She wants company, but not sex. I don't feel like listening to her for the next few hours. I'm not going to take the bait.

"Maybe you should."

I key in a request for travel, just before she takes the screen from my lap, rolls it up and tosses it on the ground. She enjoys the game of not getting the attention she wants—if it's a quick one. With a shake of her head she fluffs her hair in my face, defiant. It's not a come-on at all; I know her moods. She's a thirty-eight-year-old child—they're not hard to understand. She's been wandering around like this for two days.

"All right, tell me about the speech," she says, arms folded.

"You're incensed by the opposition's ignorance of the plight of the male," I tell her. "They seem willing to allow low sperm count and minimal-skills employment opportunities to define his—"

"Easy there. Lean positive."

I reach down and retrieve the screen, straightening it out so I can admire my handiwork. "Additionally, you find an urgent need to set aside a portion of urban reconstruction funds to include fertility research and job training that—"

"The refugees?"

"Can you wait one paragraph?"

She shakes her hair in my face again, just as a knock comes from inside the terrace window.

We both turn to see a courier open the door and step out into the light. He's young, I've seen him at parties here before. "Senator?"

"Yes?" Juliet pauses and stretches—showing it all off for the courier.

"Transport is ready."

She's surprised.

I look up, guilty. "I had to get you out of here somehow."

She gives my cheek a fond feel and shifts her focus to the courier. "No, you're right. I'll go scare up some distractions." She ties her hair back. "Are you and Margo free for an overnight?"

"Tonight?"

"Tonight."

"I think so."

"Tremendous. I've got a treat planned. We're going country."

"Do we pack?"

"The place is equipped. I want to raise some hell with you two."

"Margo was thinking about more of an urban-flavored hell for this weekend. We could catch up with you and your trouble later."

"No. Special occasion. We're going." She's like that: *No.* "Bring the speech, we'll go over it."

"I'll forward the file to you in an hour."

"Fine, fine. And tell her not to worry about being bored. We're going to the country, but we're going to burn it down."

The last time she planned a treat for us, we went to her island and were administered a fungus while listening to some sermon by her healer of the moment. We were awake for four days, euphoric. She kept the swimming pools overflowing and the cooks cooking. We were never any more than a few feet apart at any moment, always touching, but too high for any sort of release. On the last day, we were still so confident that we produced her campaign address from the beach. She swore to fight not only for her constituency, but for unity among the three parties. Her bliss came right through the screens and into the souls of the voters. And none of us felt any sort of crash from the ride down, just a slow return to normalcy that left normalcy looking a fraction better than it used to. Three weeks later, she'd won her second term. Now representing nearly a fourth of the nation, she's trying to expand her power to the west, as far as the ocean. No one doubts her. It's been six months since that weekend and I still feel a buzz at the end of the day, like there's always a gift waiting for me when I get home. I'm not sure if it's the drug or the effect of living so close to Juliet's sense of certainty.

After I finish the speech, I send it to her. I print the practical union contract for signing and go inside, walking through the inner offices, while the controlled air eases my sunbaked skin. I'll take something for that. Margo isn't at her chair. I head back to our cabin to find her.

As I walk up the path of slate circles, I glance up at our closed curtains, the signal. Out of respect, I wait on the doorstep a full minute, listening. There are voices inside— calling out, slowly finishing. This used to hurt, but the ache's gotten duller. Now it's like standing on a line. This waiting always makes my mind jump to the rational: If she did not have this freedom, I would not have this freedom; and most of all, we would never have met Juliet and would still be scrambling on the streets.

A few months into our first practical union, Margo decided it was time for me to exercise my unused rights to extra-union sex. She dragged us to a flesh club, fed me a handful of tablets and gave me an order to fulfill any fantasies. She promised to help, said it was absolutely necessary for her peace of mind, and it would free mine in ways we couldn't even imagine. I pointed out a woman who caught my eye, dancing with three other women. There were beds on either side of the dance floor and they were all occupied and glistening with some oil being misted onto the crowd.

Margo laughed at my tameness—why not all the women together? or a couple at least? how about a man?—but she accepted I was a relative beginner and steered us through the crowd toward Juliet.

The truth is that I had recognized the senator instantly and pointed to her almost as a dare. Early on, during the urban-rural battles, Juliet got famous by showing up at the front of all the protests. Well-funded by a semiconductor fortune, she kept at it, grandstanding whenever she could, waving banners, climbing on buildings, the microphone always in her hand. Then there was the image of her fist at her forehead, tears in her eyes, watching the last Barricade fall. She became the poster child for peace. Her curves never hurt the cause either. I was five years younger and, at the time, poor and permanently horny, so I thought she was God. She grew into a well-spoken diplomat for all sides, breezing her way up. Then, despite every rumor of sexual and pharmaceutical indulgence under the sun (mostly true), she was encouraged all the way up to the Senate. People seem to like their laws made by someone who has always lived beyond them. By then I'd experienced some of the world and my tastes were different. I thought she'd become a joke, an appealing one.

Margo, seeing only an attainable object, didn't notice who it was until we were already dancing with her. She gave me a proud smile as she loosened into her embarrassing/seductive groove. Juliet looked more worn than I would have thought, more glazed with skin products and diamonds, but I found myself drawn to her. Celebrity, I believe it's called.

I have no natural rhythm, which brings out sympathetic responses in women, to the extent that I've never felt the need to improve. Margo and the pills kept me at least facing my target. Juliet was amused. She read the dynamic correctly in a second and soon she and Margo, with open, voracious grins, were bumping me into a skittish sandwich. An innocent, I left Juliet to have the first words.

"Hey," she said.

"Hey," I replied.

She smiled and asked, full of flirt, "What are you up to?"

My mouth opened into unreasonable honesty: I told her that I'd achieved a high rating doing emergency work for the government, that Margo had spent time in the field as well and that we desperately needed jobs.

Stoned, she smiled blankly, as if I'd commented (as would have been appropriate) on the music. She looked Margo up and down and gave an approving nod. She never stopped dancing as she took my face in her hands and pulled it close, like a crystal ball, and slurred, "All right. You've got slim enough shoulders. You'll do." She laughed a little, either at us or herself.

After I'd compulsively bored her with my qualifications, trying to keep my feet moving the entire time, Juliet asked to see our place. We had been moving constantly for a year and were living in my grandparents' old apartment then, with some of their furniture still there. We led her in like she was an official visiting a disaster site. She looked around with unsurprised pity and then the interview began: What were we doing out that night? What were we doing with our lives? What was the status of our union? We underplayed some of the missing years in there, but she's a pro at assessing people and seemed to understand that we did what we had to. She kept her eyes on both of us, until she made up her mind.

"Gorgeous," she said, "I can use you both, you're hired."

Her driver whizzed up in her decked-out truck—couches and curtains and candy of every variety—and suddenly we were winding our way out of the city. Juliet started stripping down, urging us to do the same. We fell over each other every time the truck took a turn, laughing the whole time. There was a moment there, we were all on the couch, and I saw her drop a bracelet that was so heavy with black diamonds you could hear it when it hit the floor. Margo noticed me noticing it and put a finger over her mouth, indicating that I should keep my truth-telling mouth shut for once that night.

Now, from our pine front deck, I can see at least three armed guards. Juliet built her compound along a mountain crest, like a king would build a castle on a hill. But height alone doesn't confer protection these days, so we've got patrol in the sky too. This force is trained to notice everything, and I feel like asking the guy at the edge of the field if he knows who's in there with Margo.

A footpath slinks halfway down the hill from the cabin. I follow it, till I'm almost out of sight so as to provide whoever it turns out to be a discreet departure. Standing there, just below the rise to our cabin, trying to stay in the shade, I look over the contract. It's then that I notice the new rider on the form:

A third party may enter into a Practical Union with members of a proposed Practical Union (or with an

existing Practical Union at the time of their renewal),
provided the added party affirms that he/she will equally
support the other two parties in keeping with all of the
provisions of the contract.

This is interesting.

I look up as one of the statistics advisers leaves the cabin. Margo's been with him before. Taller than me, but he's got a paunch. Fine. I'll give her a few minutes to shower.

Juliet says falseness in others makes her throat close. At the same time, she is usually turned on when we tell her about past scams—draining water from our neighbors' tanks, hacking credit accounts, talking our way into gated towns and leaving with backpacks of jewelry and power blocks. She particularly enjoys hearing about Margo's teenage habit of seducing an attractive dealer, pulling a three-day binge with him and his goods, then turning the sucker in for a reward. Juliet assured us early on that she's more than happy to give us what we want without deception. She's made good on that. Her people wiped our records so we could be hired. They trained us in their hardware so we could work at ridiculous salaries. And just last month Margo asked her for a bigger cabin and this place was built within a week.

Still, it feels like we are always on our best behavior. We smile more than we used to. We're more alert, more thoughtful, better intentioned—when it will be noticed. My hope is that someday it will be who we really are.

The reason Juliet chose us, it turned out, is we're heterosexual. Voters are fine about ignoring her personal life, to a point. Since the various media outlets force them to read endlessly about her night crawls, which usually involve some variation of the women we danced through to get to her, they want variety of gender. In the first month, she dressed me up in rubber and had me fuck her on the main stage of just about every flesh club in her constituency—the million-dollar landscaped ones in the cities, the back-road barns in the country. It didn't matter that for the first week I was too intimidated—by her sexual certainty, by the curious crowds—to get it up, even with meds. She moaned the necessary moans to be sure word got around about her and her newest male hire. After I finally—as Margo put it—showed up for the party, I felt like I had suddenly found my appetite. Best of all, the strategy worked. In the old days, the candidate had to eat a lot of doughnuts to get their message through, but Juliet's calculations about the addition of us to her entourage were correct.

Of course, she and Margo began their affair too, though not nearly so well advertised. What I'm getting at is that every relationship is casual for Juliet, and she lets people go as easily as she has taken us on. So, if the three of us were joined together on this rider, we could guarantee our position, for at least the next year and a half. Our eager laughs might let up, and we could settle in and feel secure for a while. And for Juliet—I could check with research on this—a sanctioned steady relationship, especially adjoining an existing couple, could be good for public perception.

"Why're you hiding down there? People will gossip."

Margo, tightly wrapped in a tan towel that goes down to her ankles, is on our deck, holding an enormous goblet of white pinot from one of the vineyards here. She toasts me with a guilty smile. She's glad to see me with my shirt off, even in this unforgiving sun.

The truck has two semicircular black leather sofas in the passenger cabin. They can be locked together to make a heart-shaped bed, but tonight Juliet has the front one swiveled around to face forward with the screen down between them so she can sit there and make calls while Margo and I watch old movies in the back.

We picked *RoboCop,* a mutual favorite. The sappy story about the friendship between two cops is decent, but the futuristic stuff is interesting because they got everything so wrong. Robotics were promising and crime was grim, so they made a movie about it. But then violent crime resolved (or became part of the food distribution problem), and robotics fizzled. Next? You think you're worrying about the right thing and then you're sideswiped. *The seasons change,* as Margo likes to say, with a ton of darkness added on. She almost sings it, when she's feeling frisky enough, with this glee in her voice that someone else's dreams have disappeared.

We laugh straight through the movie, until I quietly slide her the contract, pointing to the rider about adding a third to our union. It doesn't seem to click anything for her, so I raise my eyebrows toward the front seat. Margo pauses the movie to let it sink in. RoboCop's partner is holding on for her life in a shoot-out.

Juliet is talking patiently into her mic about the necessary compromise between the Senate and agricultural organizations. She glances back at us in the sudden quiet and gives a businesslike smile.

Margo turns the movie back on and lowers her voice. "Why tie her down?"

"It's not about that."

"You'd want her kindnesses when you get sick?"

"I'd want her doctors. So would you—"

Margo stares at the screen. The personal data of one of the bad guys scrolls up before RoboCop's eyes. If only they'd been right about that prediction.

"All right," she says. "How often does she have you alone?"

"Once, maybe twice a week. Then the two of us once more, nothing regular."

I should ask the question back, but I know the answer is more.

"OK," she says, slowly, not understanding me. "What would you want from this?"

"Simple security. Wouldn't it be nice to know where we're going to be next year?" I ask. "We could become such an installed part of her public story that when she finally gets tired of us—"

"*If.* You give her no credit."

"*When.* When she does, we'll have enough experience, enough saved in our accounts, enough public exposure, to do anything."

"What does she get?"

"Tons. First, the sheer excitement of releasing a statement that she's joining together with us—a man and a woman. Imagine the response: She'd be free to pursue whomever she wants, without nearly the scrutiny she's used to—all the questions about when she's 'going to settle down.' We would be the answer."

Margo rolls her eyes, but I keep talking. "It wouldn't be a sham, we'd still be seen out with her in clubs, we would share her bed on occasion. Second—and I just thought of this—on a conceptual level, her political persona as a uniter would be solidified in the minds of the people through the sexual metaphor of our three-way union. Tri-party leadership would become inevitable."

"You're hilarious. What if she wants more from us, in exchange for the security?"

The truck jostles over a cement boundary as we turn onto a dirt track.

"She's got a dozen other people lining up to love her."

"They're ordinary staff," Margo says.

"At the end of the day, so are we."

"Speak for yourself."

I'm getting frustrated. "Why are you putting up such a fight? You know it would protect us from whatever may come."

Margo nods. Through the tinted glass is a field of tall, thin trees—just the trunks with their few spindly branches, all the color of coal, and dead from thirst. I've noticed this property on the list of holdings before. It used to be a Four Seasons, it got sold to some corporation when the weather shifted, and then Juliet scooped it up. She had the central facility with the ballrooms and spa torn down and cleared out. She refitted one of the villas as a plush retreat. Her goal, she says, is to connect the coasts and the north-south borders with great corridors of wild land—farms, forests, suburbs reclaimed by nature. One day there will be no more cities—their shells will be ghostly interruptions of the new nation, which will be composed of rural communities linked in all directions. *Even if we aren't here, the land will be: My money will keep it safe.* When the rain comes back—ever the optimist—this is where her utopia will be.

Margo looks out at the dead trees and says, "For her to take this on, it can't be our idea."

After we get to the property, Margo and I stay in the truck to finish watching the movie. As we look out the tinted window at the guards unloading crates of vegetables—one of Juliet's feasts—and water for the night, Margo launches our strategy:

"The fact of the third-person rider can be in the back of her mind for a while, but her connection with us and then *the function of the practical union as a public act* have to be underlined within the same hour for it to really hatch. Once we've shown her the possibility exists, and secured its emotional appeal through our inimitable attentiveness, we need to affirm its political logic as quickly as possible. It directly addresses her campaign needs, as even a statement of 'settled' perversion with a couple makes more sense to the electorate than the troubling image of a happy, perpetually single woman of an increasingly certain age. This will be the most difficult part. We have to act together so she feels that this is what she wants to do. And we'll just happen to have the paperwork on hand."

Juliet knocks at the window and then opens the door.

"Did the good guys win?"

We both look dumbly at the blank screen in front of us, the credits finished.

Juliet's carrying a bottle of viognier from her vineyards in the north, and three glasses together by their stems. While she climbs in, squeezing between us on the sofa, Margo pours the wine and takes the lead. "It's chilly out there. What sort of sleeping arrangements are in store for us tonight?"

Juliet rolls her eyes back briefly, hinting at some unforeseeable ecstasy she's got planned. We will alter our minds and test our bodies in some novel way, while I sit back and let it happen.

If my desperate fifteen-year-old soul were here, it would marvel at my excellent fortune. It's all been the result of my insistence on the practical union in the first place. I opted for it to protect—I thought—my heart, but Margo exploited it to expand our world. When I proposed, getting down on one knee even, she said, "If you want it, I'm going to make you use it."

Name an act, a theft, a drug, a social rung, a job, a dream: We have tried it or abstained only for reasons of health or sanity or law. The goals don't always entice me, but they entice Margo, and I will be quiet or charming or rough in order to reach them.

Juliet slides the black diamond bracelet up and down her slender wrist. "What makes you so sure we'll be sleeping tonight?"

"We are entirely at your disposal," Margo says, handing her a glass. "Here you go. And don't tell us one word about it. Keep it a surprise."

Margo passes a glass to me with a soft-eyed smile that tells me we will succeed.

Juliet takes two logs and feeds a small fire in an enormous polished black-stone fireplace. "Just for some light." She had the place done up like an English conservatory, with a half-dozen old-style globes scattered around, Persian carpets and giant potted cacti everywhere else.

We walked in, and Juliet dropped her organizer and bag onto an easy chair, telling us where we would be for the evening. As if by accident, I placed the relevant papers on a small marble table by the door to the greenhouse.

Margo looks completely at ease, as per usual, and that is part of her magic. Two years ago, we went to see my mother for what would turn out to be the last time. Gaunt by then, she had sold whatever she could find and moved to a desert town, to attend a franchised school that trained servants for the rich. She always had schemes like that, but this one, even to me, seemed like it might have legs. Mom was on her own there, with a futon and some cooking gear in a brick shack on the outskirts, a steep step down from what she was used to. No neighbors, just a table-flat view of red rock and sand. I remember envying her, though, with all that quiet sky, no big storms, just going to classes, studying and practicing all the bullshit manners. It would have been a beautiful life, if it was the one she wanted. It was all just a step for her, on some imaginary road toward stability. We hiked for a few days across a high rocky plateau, along streams and around karst castles. She loved Margo, was convinced she would save me from a life of petty crime, not lead me to it. One night we found ourselves farther out than we'd anticipated and too tired to dig for water. My mother was getting frantic—"We'll just die out here, people do every day, it's not always reported 'cause they're not always found, but we've got no resources, none!"

Margo smiled. She took her pack behind a rock and a minute later returned with a tin cup of pee. "Hydration solved," she said, raising it high, "but you should only drink your own," she said. That simple toast turned drinking our own piss into a festive occasion. She handed my mother, already calmer, an empty cup and shooed her off to the bushes. With a smile in her voice, Margo called after her,

"Drink it now, by the morning it will be too strong!" Even lost in the desert, Margo is still at home.

She pours more wine as Juliet distributes the pills. It's an antinightmare drug designed for post-trauma, which you're supposed to take before bed. She wants to see what it does if we stay awake all night. Supposedly nothing, she thinks, but if we're *conscious* and *experiencing, something will happen.*

We're waiting for dinner to be brought in. Juliet is going on about the source for the pills, a chemist she knows who studies side effects. Momentarily bored, she gravitates to the only reading material in the room, the papers, talking the whole time. Margo, by the fire, and I, by the window, pretend to listen. We remain vigilant, watching her glance land on the pages.

"I can't imagine working on paradigm-shifting medicine and being stuck on such secondary interests as side effects. Headaches, stomachaches. That's way too little picture, don't you think? End users expect too much. If you want the rainbow, you've got to have some rain."

Now curious, I open my mouth to ask, *What are the side effects for the pills we just took?* but stop before the first word because Juliet's hand lands on the first page of the contract. She raises her brow and then turns it over. She's absorbed, but has not necessarily made the connection. She looks up at me, her mind back on our conversation. "Honestly, does it matter? If we start to feel funny, we've got pills for the pills."

Dinner is served.

We sit facing the fire, eating from plates of the sweetest

carrots and peas, the richest spinach, the subtlest cucumber—
all bred in the greenhouses—and we talk about the textures
of the food, the nutrients, how all beings need sustenance.

When I get up to retrieve the wine, I'm blasted with a
headrush and suddenly I cannot imagine that the plan will
fail, that Juliet won't give us exactly what we want. Amazed at
the sudden confidence, I *try* to imagine it all coming apart,
but my mind won't even catch on the thought. The doubt
rolls off.

Steadying myself, I make my way to the cooler and see
that Juliet has brought nine bottles for us for the overnight,
twice what she usually carries. She doesn't want us to sleep
and she doesn't want us to sober up. As I sit down, tightening
our little circle, I wonder what other doubts the pills may free
us from. With a wave of clarity, the whole idea of us even having a "plan" seems pointless because what we want is clearly
what she wants too: She brought us out here to pop the question *to us*. What a moment that will be!

Margo diverts the discussion to the opposite of nightmares, daydreams. She speaks lovingly of understandable
worlds, secure situations—gently, gently massaging us toward
our goal. She mentions a wish for a cabin somewhere quiet,
a plot of fertile land, a return of seasons and all the time in
the world to watch things grow. It's news to me, but she keeps
going, elaborating with images of the three of us, tilling and
caring and harvesting. Juliet says she likes the plan, and her
cheeks go red. She opens her eyes wide as the blush extends
from her face to her body, which sets off a chain reaction in

all of us, till we've each been chilled by a full drench from our own sweat.

Margo, riding the certainty we're all on, raises her hands up in exclamation, like she's about to start a rain dance, but then lets them come softly down, one around my neck, one around Juliet's. She draws us in close: "I love you" first to me, then to Juliet. A beaming Juliet throws her arms into an open hug around us and returns the declaration, though I wonder if she's said "I love you two," or "I love you too." The question dissolves the moment it forms in my mind. I reach around and squeeze us all into a closer huddle and start the kiss. The three sets of lips press together easily as they always do; the glow on our faces, the foxlike glances in our eyes make it feel all the more urgent.

But the connection here, tonight, in this house in the forest on this parched land in this desperately healing country, is mythic. We are not merely dreaming the same dream of union; we are intended, as much as anyone ever was, to be right here right now in this single embrace that will yield nothing but positive reverberations for the planet.

Arms drift down, tracing backs, feeling bodies. I go first, grinding and pushing us together, to make more skin touch. We press back into a pile of pillows, never letting go of each other. Juliet and I focus on Margo, as she urges us to open her shirt. We silently conspire to overwhelm her, nursing at her breasts, teasing her when we take short breaks to kiss each other. Then we return to her with gentle teeth, each time coming back a little rougher. Her body is like a tiny ocean underneath us, until one of us bites too hard and she tenses.

Juliet suddenly unlatches and pushes back. She sits up. She looks down at the two of us through her messed hair, as if confused by her instincts, like an animal giving up on its prey. I have no choice but to let go. The spell feels momentarily broken. Margo looks up at us with a laughing question mark in her face, and I hear Juliet clearly say to herself, "No."

Easily, softly, so that no one would be embarrassed, Juliet reaches forward and covers up Margo's chest. "Not yet." She gives us both kindly pecks, yanking us out of our erotic haze, and commands, "Up. Follow." She's taking control and that's wonderful. As we help each other to stand, she adds, giggling, "If you can, try not to talk." She leads us out to the driveway.

Margo and I contain our thoughts and walk single file, like schoolchildren, behind Juliet out to the truck. The requisite guards are nearby but they seem to have instructions to stand down as she loads us into the front and climbs into the driver's seat. The moon is spotted silver, like an old mirror. I follow Juliet's glance to the back of the truck at three hazard suits and air tanks neatly draped across the front couch. She is going to have us walk through some adventure to prove our love. She gives a nod to a guard waiting by the garage and we drive on, continuing deeper along the dirt road. As we go, the guards seem to suddenly scatter and mobilize, as if preparing to leave. But the contract is still on the table. Wherever she's taking us, she'll surely have another.

Nobody speaks as the truck knocks through the woods.

Where we're too wide, the trees crack easily, giving us space. A branch the size of a fat man's arm falls off and onto the front of the truck with a thud. Maybe it's the drug, but we don't even flinch. Margo, in fact, starts to crack up. She tries to laugh to herself, if only because Juliet asked us to be quiet, but the comedy increases as the log rolls around as we drive. It keeps looking as if it's going to roll off the edge, but then we drive over a rock and the truck seems to tilt in exactly the right way to hold on to it. Margo loses it over this, in a near fit, and then so do the rest of us. Juliet, laughing now, gives Margo a look of concern and purposefully speeds over a rise to make sure the log falls off. Finally, with patient amusement, she gives us a firm "Shh."

We stop at a small clearing in the middle of the woods. She gets out and tells us to put on the suits. Maybe jets out of the back so we can zoom up above the trees, maybe an old mine to explore. There's always a reward. As the three of us are standing there with our suits half on, calibrating oxygen tanks, Margo starts laughing again. "I know. We can zip ourselves together, like it's one big suit."

Juliet remains patient and tries to quiet her down, but Margo doesn't stop. "Imagine how cool that would look? The three of us. Imagine. Imagine." She leans in close to Juliet's ear, "*Imagine.*" And in case she's afraid of being too subtle, Margo adds, "Like a big three-way union."

I glare at her, but she's peaking, grinning like an idiot. I zip her suit up to her neck, to jerk some sense into her. It doesn't work; she turns to Juliet: "Don't you think your persona would benefit from it? It would prove you're grown up now, but on your own terms." I stop looking at her. I pretend it's not happening because it's such a brutal deviation from the plan. Still, most of me remains unable to even panic, certain that Juliet is taking it all the right way, understanding we're all on the exact same page.

Margo grabs me by the ears and tells Juliet, "This one. He thinks he's dreamed it all up and we're going through the steps, but he's going to get the biggest surprise, right?" She winks at Juliet with a leer.

Juliet gives Margo a stern glare. "Put on your helmet, my dear delicate friend."

As Margo lowers the metal ring over her head she tells me, "You'll see. Seasons change."

Juliet rolls her eyes and says, "I don't know. The pills, I guess." She's consoling me.

I don't begin to understand the truth of what's happening here. I could at least try to process this, if my brain could only hold on to the notion that I've been hurt.

We each lock on our headgear and sync communication so we can hear each other inhale and exhale. Margo's emotional, her breath is fast and her voice is breaking up, like she might cry.

As long as I have known her, I have never known peace.

Juliet pretends it all away by looking up at the moon. Whatever her experience is now, she's not letting go of her plan for us. She slips into the slow vanilla voice she uses for colleagues, not friends. She's rational, tactful, and knows the end of each sentence before she says it. Like a good leader, she never strays too far from an even tone. "I brought you here as a present—I know the end of your union is coming up and I'm sure that you two are going to recommit. Without resorting to some loony wedding reception, I thought it deserved some recognition."

Margo has tears running down her face, she looks at me with wild joy, then back to Juliet. "Thank you."

"I want you two, with this gift that you have, to feel as sanctified as you possibly can. True love is balanced, rare, and I've never seen a more shining example."

"Where's the wine?" Margo barks. "I want to toast the three of us!"

Juliet shakes her head. "No. This is just for the two of you." There's a spark in front of us as she lights two long white candles with a match. She hands one to each of us. "Go on. We're protected." She holds her arms open to the woods. "It's time for it to go. Do the honors. Don't think about it, we're safe in the suits, the vehicle is secure, the edges of the forest are protected. Everyone, everything is safe. It will all grow back. The forest needs the fire."

Margo's eyes are shining. "Yes! Yes!" she yells, as she pushes her little flame against one twig and then another. She turns to me in lecturing ecstasy, "You don't even comprehend it, do you? She's with us all the way, this sanctity thing is just talk. We're three, we're secure, we're together. We're three already, you don't need documentation! You've got your security and all the love you'll ever need!"

The forest behind her starts to crackle up into flames. We are surrounded. We can walk out when it gets too bright, but for now the plan is to stay right here in the center of this nighttime sun. Juliet drops the book of matches at our feet and it joins the other fire with a pulse. A blast from an exploding log pushes us a step closer to each other. The sparks bounce off us and fall to the ground. Against this inferno, the candle in my hand is keeping the last intact flame. It's twitching in the wind to get out and join the rest and the candle itself is starting to wilt.

"Go on," Juliet tells me, nudging me toward a spindly branch not yet burning. I falter, pulling my elbow back toward my hip.

Margo laughs. "What's wrong, commitment problems? Just do it. It's unbelievable. Light one and they all go. Be a man! We're never going to burn!"

I hold my candle out, touch the fire to the wood, watch it catch and spread, and spread farther. As it jumps and multiplies into the world, I look at the women, their excited faces shining through all our layers of fireproof glass, and realize I no longer want anything at all.

Predisposed

All I did was ask Jeph if he would help collect branches for a roof repair today. It's what's expected of us, it's the kind of thing a normal kid might like to do on a dull afternoon. What I got was a fake sorry smile and, "Given the state of your body, don't you think it would be for the best if you got the full benefit of the exercise yourself?" Fourteen years old.

He's here with me now, though, tying up his share of branches, but with that bullshit teenage look of inner peace on his face, just to make sure I know he's not helping because he has to: It's only a favor.

Not entirely his fault that he thinks his presence is a gift. The elders encouraged free participation by the children and now that he's the last survivor of the kids, he hasn't heard the word *no* in some time.

An only child with twenty-seven parental figures, he even looks precious. Years of nighttime farming duties have left his skin bone white. To highlight the effect, he conned some-one into bringing a eumelanin supplement back from the city to keep his hair gleaming black, and he trims it every few days into a tight helmet of dark fuzz. And even when he's talking, those vague blue eyes stay crystal and distant, like he's working out some sort of math problem about you.

There's a click in the woods nearby. I turn to it, looking for a human shape. No one's there. I stare off into the cam-ouflage of leaves, hearing nothing else.

He looks at me with pity. "Nobody's after our sticks. You have got to find a way to be calm, man."

"It's in the job description."

"You won't be able to take care of any of us if you've got ulcers. You're eating yourself alive."

His nerve to address his elders like this is half privilege of being an only child in a community and half from watching too many movies on his handheld.

"I'm fine. I appreciate your concern."

"Right. Do you mean you're grateful for it, or you *understand* it?"

I look at him as if to say, *Shut up.* He folds his arms, pumping his forearms up with his fists, as if to say, *Make me.* He's in the middle of this growth spurt that has his clothes getting snug and he refuses to do anything about it because he wants us all to see—and comment on—every developing muscle. Even that's not enough for him though. As we were clearing our way through the forest this morning and I was holding branches back and waiting for him to make sure he kept up, he broke his silent treatment only once, to inform me that I have to get him a synth hormone to kick-start some serious hair growth. "My legs look like a baby's. I should look like the animal that I am."

The animal that he is. Sexually mature now, if you can call it that, he's stuck out here with no outlet at all and younger than everyone by at least fifteen years. His fantasy life is limited to a library of old sims and downloads. Besides, he assures me he's trying not to become "addicted to images of blatant sexuality the way some older men do" as he's striving to develop "along a spiritual plane, which you won't ever connect with, no matter how hard you try." Just yesterday he revealed that he's able to jerk off by thinking about the bliss of the night sky. What a fucking jewel.

He takes my glance as admiration or God knows what, because he suddenly asks, "You ever had it off with another man?"

"No."

"So you have?"

"No. I haven't."

"Should I read that as a yes?"

Looking directly at him now, "No."

"It's all right, buddy, your secret's safe with me." He jumps up, grabs onto a branch, does ten quick chin-ups, then swings down on it twice, till it cracks, bending down. He takes off his shirt and grabs the small ax with an exaggerated swagger. He steadies the tree with one hand while he hacks off the branch with the other. He flexes his biceps for me: "You like?"

"No."

"Interesting," he says, as if he still hasn't heard the truth. "Not that I'm thinking any thoughts like that, least not now, and, no, not with you. I was curious what you'd actually own up to. Not much, I guess. It's a tight society out here. I understand." He idly pulls down a branch, keeping an eye on me, while throwing the last branch onto our pile. "Is this enough wood for you?"

"It's not *for* me. It's for the community."

"Is this enough wood?"

I look around at what he's accomplished. He's productive even when he's being a prick, and we've got enough wood. I give him a nod and tell him to tie up the last bunch.

"Sure thing." He collects it, straightens it, wraps it once, then pulls the cord tight around the pile. With an angelic smile, he drops it down between us. "Here you go. Faggot."

The elders have come up with a litany of direct ways to handle his disrespect, no matter how clever it is. I'm supposed to gently explore the source of his hostility, in this case, discuss the clear sexual anxiety he's going through, dispel any fears of abnormalcy. Instead I wait him out with my own silence. I've only got him for another hour, then he's on his own until just before mealtime.

Jeph bundles the piles together and stands. "You're the one who ought to be carrying all these back. You've got to. Your bones, your muscles, they need to do some work. I'm in fine shape. It's your system that isn't thriving, my friend."

It's not that long a hike, they're not that heavy, my system is fine. I load all the bundles onto my back and head us through the woods, to our community. He's following at a petulant distance behind me, carrying nothing. I refuse to wait for him now and I'm marching through the forest, winding along the widest paths I can find. I hope he's thinking how wrong he is about my bones, but the fact is he's probably thinking about what extra food he can scam away from some of the other elders at mealtime. He is, after all, a growing boy.

Jeph's mine again for dinner prep, and we're in the kitchen peeling chickpeas. Actually, I'm peeling chickpeas. Jeph is exploring new ways to irritate.

"Do you ever wonder if your whole safety trip isn't more of a manifestation of a brain condition than a meaningful skill?"

When I moved here last year, it wasn't enough to manage security for five hundred acres of farm and forest. I also had to take on educational and emotional guidance of Jeph as a symbol of my commitment to the future. I would provide intimate counsel to help him grieve for his parents; I would offer a role model and friendship. Not sure if it's worked. If I suggest participation in community events outside of mealtimes, he wrinkles his nose. If I try to engage him in maintenance of the security systems, I get sarcasm. If I try to talk to him about his parents, not even dead eighteen months, he gives me nothing of import. He says he knows they loved him, accepts their loss and has "no understanding on why anyone else's opinion should influence the way I choose to grieve." My suspicion is no one else wanted the gig.

He goes on. "What I mean is: What if you took a neuro pill and suddenly lost all your interest in who's coming to get us? You'd relax a tiny bit. I mean, I never worry about strangers, least not till one of your dumb alarms go off."

I purposefully slow my breath and think about his value to the community. I exhale completely before talking. "There are a few pills I could take, I suppose. But one of the reasons we live here the way we do—without access to all the pills— is because we know that through plain living—"

"Stop. That's why only half of us are left."

"There are a few pills you could stand to take, my friend."

His eyes scan my face, possibly sensing my dwindling patience. He points to a freckle on my cheek and says, "You should have that one looked at." I continue working on dinner, he continues talking. "I'm going to be OK. Maybe a bit of arthritis when I'm older—my dad had it in his knees—but that's a while off. Depends if I keep farming. I don't need any pills right now, except to sort out my puberty. Honestly, I only wanted to see how you think about your future. What's inevitable, what's not."

"Why don't you strain the yogurt?"

He ignores me, naturally, and stares out the window to the far hill, where our cemetery is, where the other half of us are. He reaches for the strainer and the yogurt and finally gets working.

But he's stuck on this one. "So you accept that we're just *here,* just helpless? No—I'm sorry—that we're *simply and reverently following nature's plan.* But what if you could get

142

over that steady drip of anxiety you've got coursing through your brain? What if you cleared your mind for smarter work? If I were you, a free citizen, no personal ties, a body full of problems, I would want to save myself as much as possible. And it wouldn't be hiding out from life here. You got your heart scorched or something? That's the only reason single people ever end up here."

"What does 'body full of problems' mean?"

His gaze moves, for the first time, to the yogurt. "Nothing I can't see by looking at you."

I don't say another word until I tell him to ring the bell to call everyone to eat.

At dinner, he only draws attention to himself when he gallantly refers all thanks for the food to me. This humility is greeted like an even greater gift than the dinner itself. I realize that he's been on bizarrely good behavior with everyone else for the past few weeks. He doesn't challenge, interrupt or flirt at meals as much. To the others, it probably looks like he's got control of his hormones, like this difficult spell has passed, or even like I have somehow gotten through to him and successfully shown him the way to maturity.

At cleanup, as soon as we're alone, he asks me, "Of all the women at the table tonight, who would you want to fuck first?"

I'm silent, consoling myself with the fact that in a mere two years he'll turn sixteen and I'll be free from him.

"Hey. I'll tell you my answer first, if you'll tell me yours.

And you can include any men too, if that's what you're into."

I encourage him to take a long walk by himself. I suggest that he inspect the western edge of the security fence. I tell him there's a short circuit coming from the middle portion of the far perimeter. I suggest it in such a tone that tells him that I don't require any more of his company.

"You're not coming with me?"

"I'm going to read. You know the way. You can handle it."

"Should we get permission for this?"

The prospect of a walk alone, even if it is in the service of the community, sits well with him. The fence is fine, but he probably won't even go check it. He'll take his time, wander, be gone past ten.

"I'll take responsibility. I trust you." He can go jack off at the moon.

His room is in perfect order. For all his professed maturity, it's still a boy's room, with his range of ingenious nooks and mementos from the forest and other people's travels. I don't even look twice at the handheld, which he's triple-encrypted so no one will find his porn. Remembering what in the room I've touched and how, I go through all the drawers and shelves. If he senses this search—and if I'm wrong—he'll report the violation. I'll have to publicly apologize, there'll be a spiritual investigation and I could lose guardianship, which wouldn't be at all awful. I'm still worth too much to them to be asked to leave. If I'm right, this intrusion will be justified and he'll have no one to complain to. Win, win.

I flip through his books. No loose pages. I find an old journal. No recent entries. Nothing under his mattress. There's an aluminum can filled with thousands of dollars in old paper money tucked behind a tidily folded pile of clothes. Still, no luck. I sit on the floor in front of his desk—it's an old door lying across a metal file cabinet and a sawn-off tree stump of the same height. The file cabinet is empty except for the various old gaming units that he wants to some day rewire so they draw from our power grid. As if that would ever be allowed. I look around to see if I've replaced everything exactly. Maybe I won't be caught.

On some vestige of adolescent instinct, I lift up the left side of the desk/door slightly to inspect the hollow of the stump. Something's there. I slide the board to the side and find a folded, pink medical sheet. I wasn't wrong: He had a detailed assay run on me without my knowledge or the permission of the elders.

Male Caucasian 36 years

Exposure within North America: duration 36 years
(?other exposures unknown)

Samples: Hair: bloods unavailable

ASSAY

Integument: environmentally triggered and accelerated aging evident since age 27; left cheek presents with probable benign melanoma, expected within 12–18 months

Skeletal and Muscular: phase one degeneration evident in spine; acute phase two degeneration within five years; neck strain, shoulder strain, associated with misc traumas; knee strain associated with compensatory behavior following stressor incident; unknown genetic factors, possible pathology—long-term time frame for onset, 10–15 years

Endocrine: no abnormalities detected

Nervous: vision reduced within 36 months—postviral syndrome

Cardiovascular: no abnormalities detected

Lymphatic: compromised immune function expected; thymic carcinoma evident, expected symptomatic 36+ months

Respiratory: no abnormalities detected

Digestive: asymptomatic ulcers evident, expected symptomatic within 72 months

Urinary: progressive nonpsychological sexual dysfunction within 40 months—postviral syndrome

Reproductive: sterile—postviral syndrome

Social/psychiatric: heterosexual, experimental behavior with multiples and same sex apparent in profile; strong cognition and problem-solving, weak emotive-spiritual; tendency toward risk-taking/impatience/dishonesty when stressed; formative years yielded strong desire/ability to trust, make attachments—countered by apparent experience; optimism subnormal, conflicts with strong survival instinct; isolationist, dysthymic tendencies expected to increase with age, esp. if marked by illness; evidence of psychotropic drug use.

Prognosis: All current and expected medical conditions treatable, excluding reproductive.

I read through it again. My fingers are white, my face probably is too. So this is my new bible. I fold it and put it in my pocket, slide the board back in place. I'm done. The room looks untouched and I don't care anyway. Gentle on my bones, I get myself up, take my body full of problems, and leave. There's a warren of dark wooden corridors to go through—this is the oldest section from the original monastery—and I make it to my room without seeing anyone.

This is where they initially put me, off the central sanctuary, promising I would get one of the more private shacks down the hill. Eventually, though, it was decided that it would be better for all if I remained closer to Jeph. In exchange, they let me have the pick of all the dead members' leftovers after they had been sterilized (myself too, apparently; oh well, I didn't think children were in the cards anyway). So I stretch out on the bed and look at the four walls, my open window. Everything in this room is either dead or dying. I open the assay and square the page in the center of my chest, like I'm dressing for burial. Was I sleeping here when he plucked the fateful hairs or did he just find them on the floor?

My fingers find holes in the bedspread, some blanket that they lifted from someone else. When was I infected? Was it here? Was it that day in the desert? I thought I was healthy. Suddenly the smell of my sweat fills the room with musky anxiety. If I weren't so damn dysthymic, I would move my broken body so I could pull the curtains over the windows to keep my scent from flowing out into the night where fragrance travels fast and alerts all the night animals that are waiting to feed on fear.

I will go to the elders for guidance. Jeph will be reprimanded for his action and they will clamp down on his finances. He bragged to me once of having access to independent accounts his mother hid from the community. He said there were millions. I didn't believe him. The elders will force him to reveal all. Naturally, their concern for the community will be limited to my ability to perform my tasks and nothing will really slow me down, except maybe the cancer. As for me, they'll let me go for treatment when it's convenient. For now, I'm more useful here, with all these ticking bombs inside me. And my incipient erectile dysfunction will be a welcome relief for the few of the unions I've meddled in. What if everyone's assays were run? Would that change minds? There'd be a great rush for the road, everyone aching to repair shoulders and glands. That, I suppose, is why they don't allow it.

I'd really wanted to call this place home.

There's no way to sneak off to a clinic without involving the elders and without resources. My pathetic savings are earmarked for the common good of the community, which probably doesn't include my left cheek. They decide who needs care and when. They control the car.

Even if I smuggled a few days' nutrition and a bedroll and skipped out tonight, I doubt I could get myself to a city. Without a government grant, nonemergency care would be a long wait. I would never see the inside of a clinic. I could con, I could beg, but by the time I made the right connections my knees, my nerves, my thymus would all be screaming for care. The community would send me by then anyway, if all of the prognoses come true. I could just stay here as if I believed and it would all work out. This dead man's bed might be the best thing I have.

The only person I can even ask for help in paying for preventive treatments right now is Jeph.

The next day is a five-star seminar in patience. We work in the shade, making a door for one of the elders. We weave sticks and dried grasses together and seal it with clay. This is our only task for the afternoon and, since he's not lumbering through it, we should be done before two. When I bend down to tip more water into the clay mix, I brace myself on my knees. Jeph suggests I go easy on them.

I slowly come to standing, emphasizing the now negligible height advantage I have over him. "How did you know my knees have been hurting?"

He gives me a slight sneer, then starts one of his philosophical inquiries. "What I don't understand is this: We're all living here by choice, right?"

"Yes. Except you, actually. You were born into this."

"No. From the time I understood, I've had the option to go. My parents made that very clear to me."

Ingratiation never quite works with Jeph. "I take it back. You're well in control of your path."

"You're not?"

He seems genuinely surprised. I have to show my cards here, so I tell him, "If I need to leave, I'm actually limited by certain factors, so I could say, no, I don't have the same choice you do. But to get back to your question, yes, theoretically, we're all here by choice. What do you want?"

"Why would you 'need' to leave?"

"Circumstances."

"I don't understand. There are no individual problems for you. You signed the covenant when you came here, didn't you? You have *earnest faith* in the process. You will allow the community to address all *circumstances,* allow time to *heal* all wounds, right? Didn't you sign something like that?"

I feel like he's turning my arm up behind my back. "Yes."

"You're man enough to stay with that, aren't you, man?"

"Yes."

He looks so disappointed in me. "What I don't get is why does everyone here lie to each other all the time? It seems juvenile. The truth comes out anyway. But it's like most of the people here can't even help it. Look at you, every time you've opened your mouth today has been a lie."

He waits for a response, but I agree, trying to look for a way out of this. "Maybe not everyone speaks with the exact same precision that you demand."

"That's all you've got to offer, an excuse? The truth is the truth and that's all there is. The sooner it's in the open, the better. You're supposed to be someone I look up to."

For the remainder of the morning he works with his usual sarcastic enthusiasm. He finds a trowel and smooths the clay down, even pressing into it a faint pattern of decorative semi-circles, a dozen setting suns in red mud.

I lie: I thank him for his help. I pretend that his care is appreciated even though I know he's doing it to humiliate me in some subtle way. He returns the lie, "It's nothing."

We carefully carry the door, still fresh and bending from the weight of the clay, positioning it on a flat rock where it can spend the next few hours drying. I'm saying nothing. Finally, disgust gets the better of him and he asks, "All right, so what are you going to do about the assay? I gave you an in before and you fumbled. Are you going to take action or are you cool with letting nature take its ugly course? The suspense here is excruciating."

Originally, I wouldn't have imagined bringing him along. He's got his mother's account as well as the paper money, which we can always sell to collectors if we need to. My only plan was to hope the elders would be lenient with me. He had another plan and it was, as he put it, as convincing as cancer. He's figured out the best hour of the night for leaving. He suggested the note, in his writing, apologizing already for the disobedience, promising to return—establishing my alibi and clearing a way for our forgiveness. The Amish, he wrote, allowed their children a year to explore the world outside; all he wanted was a few days.

For driving him to the city, showing him around, for teaching him to drive as we go (we'll see about that one), he won't mention the clinic, so no one will think that I was along as anything more than a chaperone. We'll recharge the car, bring back meds and food and batteries. He will tell them that that part was my suggestion. We will be reprimanded, we will be forgiven and then we will be adored for whatever we bring back.

After an hour, we finally drive clear of the forest and the starless night opens up in front of us. Jeph leans his face against the car's window, a fog appearing and disappearing with each breath. There's nothing to see.

We move past a dusty strip of roadside farms all growing the same spindly, shadowy crop, and finally see some activity.

Looks like one company owns them all, sentries guarding the crews and the water trucks, the fields lit up like a night game. Even though I tell him not to, Jeph stares. They stare back, guns trained.

I would never have made it through here on foot.

He's enjoying the ride, taking everything in. I ask him, "Why did you do it?"

"The assay? You're my protector, right? Just looking after you so you can look after me."

Suddenly he's not so interested in honest discussion. He did it for control, for a way out, and it worked.

He's looking behind us now, watching the farms sink out of sight. The presence of real guns seems to sober him. "My father told me there were weapons."

Jeph's quiet for the next few miles, looking at the road ahead of us, making a tough face that he probably stole from an old Western.

I ask him, "Why did you have my assay done?"

"Curious."

"You wanted something on me."

"That's not true."

I let it sit. It is true. He knows it.

"I want to drive."

"On the way back."

"You stink."

"We want to make sure we get to the city, access the credit, get to the clinic. And I don't stink, I'm taking a big chance. You're a kid. I might lose real rights. So might you."

He leans back into the faded yellow blanket draped across

the passenger side and asks, "What are they going to do anyway, fire me? And don't pretend to worry about me, you're saving yourself. Just let me do the talking when we get back and we'll be fine."

I probably should let him do the talking. He saved my life by doing the assay, and he's saving it again now by making this trip possible. I pull over.

"OK. Drive."

"Mean it?"

I walk around the car, open the door to the passenger side and shove him across to the wheel.

We speed past abandoned developments, swerve around holes in the road and briefly screech to a normal pace as we get to each crossing. He tells me he's "deep in it," tense with concentration and hungry for the next obstacle, like he's racking up points the whole time. I would fear for this recently saved life of mine, but in fifteen minutes he's already got complete control. It's pure motion for him now, matching reality to all his solitary nights of gaming. Makes me think I should see if there are still any flesh clubs around when we get to the city. Then we'll see how far he can go there, based on all those nights of spiritual practice.

As a flare of sun peeks up behind the haze of skyline in the distance, he sits straighter. He looks at me.

"Now what? Tell me where to go."

"Take this sick old man to a clinic."

He laughs, putting one arm up against the back of my seat, like we've been driving together for years. It doesn't look natural.

"Can't we do the city part first?"

"No. It's too early. There won't be anything to see for a few hours." Another lie: It's six a.m. and the markets are already shuffling to life, with every imaginable item for sale, but I want to get to a clinic before he gets distracted.

We follow signs to a medical complex outside the city ring.

We make it past security without any challenges from Jeph. He's as awed and docile as he can be, but clearly no one believes that such unwashed individuals would be able to afford treatment. At the main desk, a young blond functionary with cat eyes scans the money, verifies it and raises her eyebrows. She gets up, clips a credit note to the assay sheet and asks us to follow her into a waiting area. She's wearing an absurdly short skirt that might enhance the office environment during daylight, but at this early hour makes the place look like a meat market. Jeph watches all of my interactions with this girl with horny wonder. She asks him to sit. He sits. He looks around, trying to mask concern about being abruptly abandoned in this sterile room—empty except for a drugged old man in a corner sitting with a mangled hand.

When the woman points me down toward the care rooms, I feel irresponsible for leaving Jeph alone out here.

"Hang tough," I tell him. He looks up at me, and I can almost see fear in his smile.

I am worked on by a series of specialists who assure me that everything can be done here, there's no need for a hospital visit. They fix me up fast, zapping my insides, twisting my bones, applying transdermals. The last doctor tallies up the bill, which he flashes up to the front desk. He hands me a package containing extra meds (for the thymus; turns out it's one of the simple cancers) and a folded page describing a few exercises I might do to speed my healing. He confides, "After all the medication you've just taken, these are merely an extra tool to use, if you want to. Makes clients feel they're part of the process."

Jeph is leaning over the main desk, chatting and leering at the assistant, who is beginning-of-the-shift bored and easily amused. When she notices me walking out from the rooms, she straightens up and pushes back from her desk with a cheery swing. "Right as rain now?"

The man with the mangled hand is arguing with an unsympathetic-looking woman in a lab coat. The blonde rolls her eyes at us with uncomfortable disgust, making it clear he doesn't have the funds. I look at Jeph with genuine thanks.

"Right as rain." I raise my brows, hoping that he might pay for whatever the old man requires. Jeph gives a firm shake of his head.

"That's absolutely terrific," the blonde says, tapping the receipt on the counter. "And I sorted your son out with a little fix for his puberty. Just to speed it along for him."

Jeph widens his eyes coyly at me while semisubtly massaging his crotch.

"Whatever he wants."

She nods, reminiscing. "These years can be so tough on kids."

The woman sits back in her chair, musing at the two of us. "Your boy was charming me with tales of your adventures on the road. If I were you, I wouldn't mind too much what others say, I think you're giving him a truly rich life. It's a vital time to see the world. Vital."

Walking to the car, Jeph stays quiet and keeps his eyes on the cracked pavement. He knows enough to hand me the keys and get in on the passenger side.

"We're going to the city, right?"

"As promised."

The car starts with its usual click and shifts silently out of the lot. Before we're back on the main road, he's already started. "You heard her, it's a vital time."

"We'll leave before midnight. Get back by morning."

He starts musing. "I suppose it'll be a new kind of lie from now on, won't it? Your health. We just changed your use-by date, in case you didn't notice. The elders will start falling apart in a few years and you'll be there to pick up the slack. In ten years you'll run the place—if everyone's not dead, of course. A pleasant way to end up, a farmer, a collectivist. Isolationist, I think that's called."

A mother and daughter come into view. They're walking on the side of the highway in front of us, heading toward the city, dragging small suitcases on wheels. From a distance, they're both so neat you'd think they were wheeling down a plush corridor, not the shoulder of the road. When they hear the tires, they turn together and look hopefully in our direction.

Jeph says, "Look: One for you, one for me."

The mother glances at our faces behind the car's blue glass, assessing possible danger. In the quick frame I have of her as we pass, she looks quite savory. She's got short messy hair that's somehow perfect, and that V-shaped mouth that always lures me in. Suddenly it occurs to me that maybe she's not the mother. Maybe she's stuck in her own situation too.

I drive on, watching in the rearview as she uses her free hand to keep her shirt from blowing above her waist.

Jeph says, "You virgin. I can't believe you let them go."

"We're just going to the city, going in and going out. There are enough dangers there without picking up passengers."

A claustrophobia sets in as I start speeding along toward the city. A brown haze is already visible, the nondescript skyline coming into view. Since we don't have water with us, we'll have to stop soon. I'm scared of even that interaction with outsiders. It's been so long.

The land on either side of the road is a rain forest compared to what we've been driving through. They extrapolated some environment-resistant leafy plants to put in here as an air filter for the city, so they keep this section well irrigated. It goes on for miles. I look at Jeph, his hands on the console, his head rocking with anticipation.

"What if it gets to be midnight and I don't want to leave?" he asks.

"We're going back. If you say that again, we'll go back right now."

He leans into the blanket, rubbing his face against it, keeping his eyes on the road. In a soft, serious voice he says, "I'll tell them you forced me to come to the clinic with you so you could get at my parents' money."

This sinks in.

He nonchalantly looks over at me. "It's kind of what really happened, when you think about it. No need to make any decisions now. I might not like it in the city. But I might. Or I might want to drive around the country for a few weeks. Let's just see what happens."

This is my future. There is no choice.

I tell him, "Here, take the wheel."

"Why?

"I'm feeling flushed, I've got to get out of this jacket."

He manages to steer, while I take my time getting out of my jacket. He's too transfixed by the road to notice as I grab a wad of his paper money from the seat and stick it into my pocket. This is going to be a long day. Lucky for me I just got a clean bill of health.

I start scratching my leg, tapping my foot on the accelerator. We're jerking all over the road. It makes him appropriately uneasy. "What are you doing?"

"They said some of the topicals they gave me could cause this. I'll be all right." I tap more.

"Can't you keep your foot steady?"

"No, sorry, it's like a tremor. Why don't you slip yours over and help out?"

"I can't drive from this side."

"Sure you can. Scoot closer." I bring the jacket around my shoulders, squeeze myself closer to my door.

We're swerving badly until he manages to steady the car. I'm looking at a sandy edge coming up. I wait till he's got his foot firmly on the accelerator before I say, "Look, maybe you should just drive."

Then I open my door, relax my body, cover my head with the jacket and hope I can roll.

The sound is suddenly deafening and I've overshot the sand and landed in some shrub, before he's even wrapped his mind around what's happened. He screeches to the side of the road. I scramble to the far edge of the shoulder, under the barrier of plants so he can't see me. He's stopped the car, losing time trying to figure out how to reverse it. I can see him struggling with the controls.

I roll down into the fake jungle. I wait. Silence. I look myself over. Barely a scratch.

I stay down low, but I can hear him walking. He's calling to me, "You've got to come out. We'll go back, I promise."

The voice is far off, but slowly comes closer. He's full of

promises now, he'll behave, he's sorry, we can work together and do great things. I'm waiting for his pleas to descend to tears. It doesn't happen. It will never happen and that's why I'm down here, up to my ankles in black mud, and he's up on the road by himself. It feels good, it's where I belong: I've escaped. After a few minutes more he stops calling to me. He's not desperate at all. There's silence for another minute or two and the sound of him walking away.

I don't move a muscle until I hear him click the car back into drive and continue on toward the city.

The Profit Motive

This is an era of violence. Border clashes, the flu, the weather, and all the migrations they caused—none of it has fostered anything like camaraderie. Friends turning friends in, families dumping their sick. Small-town mayors executed for being in charge at the wrong time, some drawn and quartered by cars. The news went out about the truce three weeks ago, but that hasn't stopped hunger, so anyone with access to food (or means to get it) is still vulnerable. As I was walking here, I heard about a mob driving up to one of the larger protected settlements and blinding fifteen soldiers with chemicals, just so they could take their weapons. Old-style hatred is back.

The call for applicants advised us to be discreet, so we wouldn't endanger ourselves unnecessarily on our way to this meeting point. All our geopolitical partners and an eager explosion of committees are working hard to make the new government viable. So the word went out to public servants of previous administrations who haven't participated in interstate insurgency, who haven't been convicted of thefts of goods or currency or anything worth more than half a million dollars. Of that proud and happy few, whoever has a proposal for a fundable project and can get themselves here without being killed has a chance of landing in a very sweet spot.

The one-screen proposal that I submitted and they approved was succinct and emotionally holistic. I even used some of the soft language of care and reconciliation that this new coalition and I, it turns out, believe in.

When I arrive at the base, the guard holds out a chip of aluminum with a number pressed into it (2215) and a key. "For your valuables," she says. I'm not even carrying a jacket, but she puts the key into my hand anyway.

Once my name has been ticked, entered, another guard directs me toward a fascistically manicured lawn. The green practically glows with hybridized vitality and looks absurd after the miles of parched plains you have to pass through to get here. The grove opens out between two landscaped hills down to a valley cradling a shell-shaped amphitheater that was no doubt constructed for the occasion. It's full of other people like me, all here for an interview.

I walk halfway down the steps toward the stage to find a reasonable spot to park myself until they start calling our numbers. Even after all the dramas, the crowd of former government employees still looks like a crowd of government employees—badly dressed, badly groomed and grumbling disconsolately among themselves. There's a relief to being within a guarded compound and a bigger relief that if we can manage to appear as our best, most civic-minded, selfless selves, we should be able to score jobs out of this.

As I'm settling in for a long wait, a low whistle of feedback comes up from the ground, followed by a woman's clear voice over the sound system requesting, "2215, please report for interview." I pull my number out and double-check. It's me.

The applause is scattered at first, then grows fuller, as everyone realizes that the interviewing has begun. The whole crowd joins in as I descend, making the moment even more surreal. The cheers practically lift me toward the stage. If I were them, I'm not sure I'd be able to suppress my jealousy enough to clap for somebody else right now, but in its big collective heart the crowd is just happy. The country has stability again and overseas investors behind us. There may be enough jobs for everyone here. For a moment I feel guilty about being first up, but the sound builds to a near-deafening drum roll as I reach the acoustic center of the amphitheater, and my shame dissolves under a joy that tells me that my hard times have been recognized and maybe I even deserve to be the first. People on every level are standing now, to catch a glimpse of the fortunate citizen. It's a storm of approval, even if they're full of envy right now. It doesn't matter: The applause isn't for me. It's for the new nation.

At the height of the clapping, an effervescent and overweight administrator wearing an orange toga floats across the floor in front of the stage to meet me. The fabric twists around and up as a warm breeze dips through the theater. She's pretending to ignore the cheers of the masses, but by the time she greets me in front of the bottom step, she's beaming as much as anyone here. Her hair is an amusing teal and her face—busy eyes and lips fighting back a smile—tell me that she's feeling momentous too.

She's got a chain hanging around her neck with a few keys and a watch that jangles as she moves. Tucking a locked metal folder under her arm, she takes both my hands in hers, and grips my fingertips warmly. "My name is Karuna. Welcome. We're glad you were able to come."

"Thank you. It's an honor. A great day."

She doesn't concur, but gets to business: "The key?"

I hand her the key I was given, which she uses to access my file. She quickly gives it a scan, as the clapping continues.

Suddenly she looks up. "We can begin." She leads me toward a doorway at the side of the stage, as the applause finally breaks apart and becomes a triumphant roar. With a glance at the crowd, she says, "Doesn't feel bad being the first one called, does it?"

I look around at a sea of people looking at us. "Everyone here is lucky."

She tilts her head at this, giving a slight smirk at my political answer, and puts her hand gently on my wrist. "Just relax," she tells me as she leads me into an elevator and presses SUB5. "Stay yourself." I look at the indicator and it shows that we're going down. It feels like we're holding absolutely still. I glance at her and see her pull her shoulders up, back and then down, as if she's stretching or getting ready for a boxing match.

"The committee has endorsed the substance of your proposal. It's similar to a few other options we've been considering, but your past—well, it's just the scope they're looking for."

"I've got more details to my plan, but I wanted to keep it—"

She stops me with a long, serious blink. "What you sent is three hundred percent perfect, for now. Trust me, when they get to acting on it, there'll be time for coloring in the finer points."

"Yes."

My years as an unambitious bottom-feeder were just productive enough to keep my criminal record within acceptable ranges for any position in the new regime. If asked, I will tell her that it was never a conscious wish to become a criminal. It was an apocalyptic choice. I'm not so morally resurrected that I mean it was a choice with apocalyptic consequences; I mean it was a good choice for the apocalypse, but now I'm ready and eager to go back to work toward happier times.

The elevator doors open onto a cool airless acre of storage shelves, each one filled with rows of neatly labeled file cartons, the kind they used to use for paper files. "I believe you're over here," she says and heads off down a corridor.

I let her lead the way and resolve to have her do more of the talking.

"Nobody makes these boxes anymore. A sweeper for one of the new committees got his hands on a warehouse of them and sold them to us for nothing. They're ideal for our needs. Waste not, you know." She regards the numbers written on the boxes as we walk through a center aisle. She glances at my key again and says, "Wait here and I'll find yours."

She keeps talking as she's tracing the labels down an aisle, "You were tapped because of your work in past administrations. You've worked hard. Kept your nose clean. Except for a few missing years—which, in my private opinion, all but the most suspect of us have had. I'm sure whatever you got up to during that time would qualify you as, at the very least, 'creative.' Am I wrong?"

She doesn't wait for a response. She stands on tiptoes and manages to coax a carton off a high shelf with her fingertips. She catches it and brings it out to me, balancing it on her palm. "Here. There's only one. Sorry. We'll go through it later." I take the box as I follow her down another aisle.

She goes on, "Nothing like those missing years, eh? We're both alive, and it looks like we're both safely on the inside again, so that's what matters at the end of the day, right?"

"I did what I had to do then, but I was younger." The less I say about my time prying jewelry off bodies in hospitals, selling counterfeit government credits for food and a dozen other antistate activities, the better.

We end up at a small glass conference room at the end of the hall of boxes. The air is sealed and has been fragranced with baked something—muffins. I wonder if they checked sources and piped it in especially for me, or if they just use muffins for everyone. The room has a Gothic-arched metal ceiling that seems designed to absorb sound. "We're secure here," she says as she closes the door.

We sit down opposite each other in scavenged mahogany dinner chairs and I put the box on the too-low metal table between us. I wouldn't have expected repurposed goods here, but I suppose it's consistent with the conservative budgets.

"Maybe this will be a good place for us to talk about my proposal."

Reaching around either side of the carton, she takes my hands. Hers feel stiff and arthritic, and a blotchy tattoo peaks out from her sleeve. I wonder what she was up to during her missing years. I look up and realize she's peering into my face. It's not exactly a warm gaze. She's still for a moment, as if she's waiting for a twitch or some indication of knowledge that I don't have. When she doesn't find what she's after, she lets go of me and sits back. She glances at the arch above our heads then back to me.

"I remember your proposal. You've figured out the spirit of the coalition and you got it into words. You're a supportive team player. Entrepreneurial. It's most of what we need from you."

"Thank you. Yes."

"Yes," she mimics, with a teasing friendliness. "Now open your damn box. I hate suspense."

We both lean forward as I lift the lid.

It's my old work boots and a pair of jeans I took from a

high school locker. There's a dress shirt that never fit in there too (its source was a quiet suburban street at the end of the day, a broken window). My dog-eared copy of *Ragtime* and a psychology book I always meant to read. Also, a pocket media player, and, underneath it all, in someone's ostentatious display of good citizenship: seven hundred dollars in paper money. Things I left behind from a few of the quick exits I've had to make.

She sits back, watching me. I sit back, keeping her gaze, like a good candidate. Again, she looks briefly at the ceiling, which must hide a camera.

"These are yours, aren't they?"

"Yes." I sit still, not sure what is expected. All I want is an hour alone in that storeroom with all those other boxes so much more valuable than mine. That, and a few suitcases to haul out a decent load, a bribable guard and I'd be set.

"What's up, then? Touch them. I've been reuniting people with their possessions for seven months and I've never seen anyone not dive right in. Every piece has been sterilized. Go ahead."

This was a test that I've somehow bungled. Being too late to do anything abrupt, I move forward slowly and reach for the boots, acting as if I'm awestruck by the coalition's generosity. These items feel good to touch, natural to me. I look up at her and, briefly, at the ceiling, as if to say thank you. "I didn't understand that these were saved for me. It's wonderful."

She seems relieved as I embrace my jeans, fingering the stitching, admiring details I'd never admired before. These would trade for a fortune now at one of the city piers, and with the shirt, I could eat for a month.

"No reason to thank. We have crews, as you well know, who go through after emergencies. Sometimes they're able to retrieve potentially important mementoes to help individuals reclaim themselves as we all go about rebuilding."

"You must make a lot of people happy."

"Honestly?" She gives a meanish snort, as if discussing lesser mortals. "Some aren't strong enough. I've seen a brass thimble leave them in tears."

"That must be hard," I reflect, a little obviously.

She doesn't say anything but massages the inflamed knuckles on her hands for a minute. Then, in a lowered voice, "You've worked on this side of things before, haven't you? Hoping to do right by your clients while your own life is on the edge of calamity."

"I used to—"

"So you know how it gets: You stay professional. Anyway, all our lives are big dark disasters." She steadies her eyes on the box.

I cannot agree (and question the optimism of my potential employer) or disagree (and aggravate my assessor). She sees my polite hesitation and sympathizes. "You and I are on different sides of what we have to keep pretending is a very high fence. You and I *know* it's not really that high." She breathes and looks away from me, waiting for the cloud to pass. "Go on. See if the rest of it still fits. I don't mind."

I examine the shirt first, explaining that I must have lost weight—and, if she looks closely, length in my arms.

"Put it all on," she urges. "I'd like to see them on."

I roll up the sleeves. As I pull off my boots, I see her notice the hole in one sock. I drop my synthetic slacks and she seems to be drifting away from me. I'd feel more at ease if she, or whoever else is watching, were simply inspecting my body and not my actions. I've made it my work to eat as often as possible to stay fit. When presented with a long night in a secure environment, I do my exercises. There are scars on my hip, neck and all over my calves, but I still look scrappy enough to scare away most would-be attackers. My body is symmetrical, reasonably strong and, as Karuna pointed out, still here.

As I pull the jeans on, her eyes seem to smile with a sort of approval for my actions.

Suddenly she waves her hand at the door. "All those boxes back there. We don't know who's alive and who's not. We didn't know who was going to make it today."

As she says this, I see her eyes go teary. I quickly chime in, "I'm glad I could." I am about to change the topic to my proposal, the attractiveness of the amphitheater, whether it looks like rain, anything, when she bursts out with, "You know I lost my children at the last Barricade. Seven and nine."

The time for polite deflection has officially passed. Now fully dressed in my old stolen clothes, I sit down and assume listening posture. Lean forward on my knees, cup my elbows in my hands. As she tells me what she needs to tell me, I keep my eyes and my heart, at least theoretically, open to her.

"They had become—the four of us had become, actually—asthmatic. Like everyone."

171

I nod.

"The air wasn't controlled where we lived and—I shouldn't—"

"Karuna"—always say their name—"I'm human, tell me." As concerned as I am about the status of my grant, I know that for my own spiritual growth, and for the new coalition, I must support this stressed fellow citizen and be compassionate. "Please."

She seems reassured and continues. "It was in the first wave of losses, when they still had the courtesy of counting casualties. Gotta love that word, *casualty*. From *casual*, of course. As in, *a chance occurrence*. What my daughter might have called a whoopsy. In any case, the Barricade came up, we couldn't get meds. Wasn't going to last long, the Senate would straighten it all out. Months. We used up our whole supply, then we just followed the health department suggestions to 'take it easy' until the situation resolved. One dusty day my little boy went, the next bad day my little girl went. Done." With dry eyes she tells me, "I thought it was the worst I would ever feel, but it was just the entrance to a cave. I was very illegal for a time there, taking anything, selling anything to anyone. *Anything*. I just couldn't care." A pause I'm probably supposed to fill. "My partner and I went separate ways. We stay in touch, but there wasn't much left after the kids."

I still don't know the right words to say because, bizarrely, it doesn't seem like telling me any of this hurts. Maybe she's been advised to make this speech to all of us as some sort of

172

therapy, to encourage us to exorcise our traumas. I remain in my position, eyes soft and my face respectful, polite and resolutely silent. This is either a test or she's become unhinged and inappropriate. I nod sympathetically until she falls quiet too and there's only the faintest hum of the absolutely temperate subterranean air supply. Again, she looks at me meaningfully and I try to return the meaning, desperately telegraphing my sympathy, my own knowledge of loss and a tiny percent of my desire to get on with whatever remains of this interview. Suddenly she claps her hands together and stands up.

"Take your things with you, we'll move you along."

I stand up to change back into my more ingratiating clothes, but she stops me. "They're yours again. Keep them on," and it sounds like an order.

"Thank you." I resist the urge to look up. "Is there someone else I should thank?"

"Look," she tells me, "you'll feel better and, honestly, I'll feel better, if you stop worrying about making such a fucking good impression."

Karuna takes me aboveground in an elevator that deposits us in a small red guard's house. We're outside, behind the amphitheater, away from crowds and, one hopes, cameras. A few guards in the distance mean we have this bright field to ourselves all the way to the fence.

She's brought me here to get me to be candid with her. It's

been months since I've felt this safe outdoors. I catch a whiff of my shirt. It's like they washed it in a river and dried it on a clothesline in the sun.

I tell her, "This smells better than it ever did under my care. How did they sterilize it?"

"No idea. I'm not part of that step." She shrugs. "Now, I'm wondering: What did you enjoy the most during your lost years?"

"I was able to see a lot of the country. Meet a lot of people."

"So you like travel and you like people. Hmmm . . ." She opens her palms to the air and raises her brows, daring me to do better. She wants it. We're outside in the sun on this glorious lawn. I'll go for broke. I say, "I'll tell you. Every now and then I enjoyed being a thief. Figuring out how to get by."

She clutches her toga and pulls it forward, tightening it against her hips. I immediately backpedal: "It wasn't a crime spree. There were honest jobs in there and I didn't live luxuriously. I helped out those who were less fortunate whenever it was safe."

"Calm down. We never found a significant record." This almost sounds like criticism. I'm hurt.

I tell her, "I didn't file a report every time."

She allows me one admiring smile, and I feel a favorable shift. She's found what she's been looking for.

"Is this all part of my assessment?"

She idly pokes her thumb into her belly, clearly bored by my inability to see the larger picture, and only tells me,

"Yes and no." I'm silent, hoping for more, which doesn't come.

"Understand this: You are completely, and I mean *completely,* among friends here," she says as she grabs the cuff of my stolen shirt and leads me back across the field to the guard house.

We take stairs down this time. Karuna presses her palm flat onto a pad on the concrete wall, waits for a click, and we reenter the enormous storage room through a side door. She ushers me in quickly and holds her arm out against my chest to keep me close to the wall as we pass around orange security beams.

"Is it all right for us to be here?"

"It's unusual, let's leave it at that, but your honesty sparked me. We're supposedly under a new paradigm now, they tell me, and they say I have to *honor* what feels appropriate."

Keeping me close in tow, she navigates us through the high corridors of other people's stuff. We end up at a corner wall, at the end of a row of empty shelves. She points up, to one lone carton on top of the rack and has me take it down for her. It's heavier than mine was, and marked UNMATCHED.

With a daring smirk, she waits for me to open it.

"But it's not mine."

"I hereby authorize you."

Inside, it is a treasure chest—filled with jeweled watches, earrings, gold chains and rings—a fortune, all lost or forgotten, all homeless. The people who still trade in this kind of thing would swoon.

"Pour it out," she tells me. "Go ahead, there's no surveillance in this aisle. That's why we're here."

I look up once more for permission, before I settle into enjoying the feeling of spilling it all onto the floor. I see the diamond watch right away and, as opposed to my reaction to my boots, I instinctively reach for it.

"Good," she says. "You found something of yours?"

"It wasn't originally mine," I say, and stop, trying to imagine how to describe the particular robbery that brought it to me.

She holds up her hand, "Don't. It belongs to you as much as it belongs in this box."

She puts her fingers to her chin and pulls the skin. "I have a confession. I stole it from you. From your box. I'm sorry, it was nothing personal. I've stolen from everybody in the first three rows. My partner, we're still in touch and he's not on the inside these days and not doing so well. He needs my help every now and then."

"What?"

She looks away, ashamed. "Of all the things you leave behind in life, who really expects a watch like that to turn up again? It was all condemned or quarantined. And how am I to know how many of these citizens are still alive to even turn up to collect? No one knows about this box but us."

I am as broke as I have been in my life. I decided when I came here, though, that I'm too old for theft. This was my one chance to get back onto the good side of the ledger. Now

I'm next to my interviewer looking down at a pile of what she's telling me are untraceable goods. I am lost.

"You were able to be clear with me today," she says. "I appreciated it." She embraces me. Her toga floats out and she surrounds me in a hug, her slow doughy breath warm against my cheek. "You're just like me." I inhale, as if emotional, and I smell some medicinal lotion. Not bad, just antiseptic. This poor woman has been forced by illness into this role she's not ready for. I feel sorry for her, sorry for everyone for a moment, and try to appear suitably distraught.

Her breathing becomes shaky as she gets close to tears. "It's too much. I shouldn't have shown you. You don't need this." She clutches me tightly, "Life's just been so damned unfair for so damned long I'm not even sure of what's right."

What do I do? Should she see tears? I exaggerate a shudder to let her know that I'm kind of in sync. It seems to help. She pulls back, widening her eyes, so that her damp lashes separate and she focuses on me, the candidate she's been looking for all along. She reaches both hands out to mine and wraps my fingers around the watch.

"Take it."

"I wasn't expecting anything like this today, and if your partner needs—"

"It's *yours.*" Then, with a quiet nudge, she points to the pile. "Take two, if you like. I won't tell."

"If I get the posting I'm here for, I won't need goods for trade." I flash a hopeful look at her indicating that at some point I'd really like to return to the interview.

Her warmth drains away. "You're not judging me, are you?"

"No."

With tears still on her cheeks, she switches to a restrained fury. "If you're storing this detail so you can have an angle on me later, you don't have the right thinking for the job, I'll let you in on that tiny secret right now."

"I'm only taking care of myself. I don't need anything but this job."

"You're lying. We know you do. That's why you're here. You've got debts. We all owe somebody. Take it." She kicks a turqoise necklace across the floor. Her face looks so completely hurt, as if she's the one on the outside of this very high wall.

It's too much. I say what is probably the first honest thing in this whole process, "I'm sorry. I do need it. I want it. But I don't want to hurt my chances. I don't know what to say."

A sharp low tone fills the air for five seconds. Karuna rolls her eyes and sighs with a schoolteacher's disgust. She directs me, by pointing, to the pile of goods and the box. "It hurts for me to bend. Would you mind?" she asks.

I pocket the watch and sweep everything else back into the box. As I'm at her feet, brushing hundreds of thousands of dollars back into the carton, she tells me, "It's time for your review."

. . .

If my sense of underground direction is correct, we are now close to the first door I came through from the amphitheater—not a good sign. My reviewers are a thin man and similarly thin woman sitting in matching metal chairs with their hands in their laps. Old-school military types, they look permanently unimpressed and don't get up when we walk in. Karuna introduces me to them, Francis and Jeannie. They each dip their heads one centimeter as introduction. Karuna directs me to stand just inside the doorway as she sits down with the others facing me. It is a group review.

They watch me, studying my face, my posture. They say nothing. If only I had taken a mere fistful of what she offered me. Finally, Francis opens his geometric jaw and says, "We're impressed."

"I'm glad. If you want to discuss my proposal—"

"You have consistently, when practicable, worked for your living, in both rural and urban communities. On several occasions you adapted to what some might call catastrophic changes in your immediate world. Through these times, you have generally maintained your hopeful outlook and your health. You have managed to survive without excessive theft. You have exhibited a range of genuine honesty, kindness and patience that are exactly in keeping with what this coalition endeavors to make global." With an impressed gleam, he says, "You have something of the businessman about you," in a way that sounds like a compliment.

"Thank you."

"And your interview today largely confirmed what our

records indicated. You were at various times monitored and your limbic responses were found to be consistent with your spoken responses." How long have they been watching? Have they ever not been watching? "When they weren't, they were considered and appropriate. Your motivation-action alliances are direct. You are hard-pressed to truly lie and we do not feel you would take advantage of resources belonging to the coalition or other citizens. You may keep the watch, although it has been noted that it isn't yours."

Jeannie stands up. She sharpens her brow and almost looks past me as she talks. "The issue of honesty is critical. We are at a crossroads and need to assure our partners that we intend to conduct business in a transparent manner."

It's come up twice now and I can't help myself: "I thought the notion of 'business' in government was no longer current."

She gives Francis a sideways, told-you-so sneer.

Karuna jumps in. "He may not be up-to-date with the glossary. It's just words. You two can let it all go. He understands what's needed."

Not entirely convinced, Jeannie continues, "Indeed. Do you intend to be cooperative and compassionate?"

She makes it sound less than fun, but I say, "Yes."

"Do you feel that you can conduct yourself honorably at all times?"

I solemnly nod, not thinking about what she might mean. I am proud now that I refrained from a second dip into the goody box.

"And, with the goal of the social good, are you prepared to expect and enforce such conduct among all citizens?"

I nod again. Karuna is looking to my side, trying not to look at me. I balance my feelings, again, exhibiting no conflict.

Jeannie's face brightens into a crooked smile, she says, "I'm done," and turns it back to Francis.

"Final question then. Is there anything you would like to tell us about today?"

"No."

"About the interview?"

I shake my head, trying to stay level inside.

He pushes it. "Anything you may have learned about your interviewer that might be relevant to the parameters we've outlined?"

Karuna is biting her upper lip, trying and failing to look natural. She is one sentence away from losing her position and her face is white. I could enforce compassion or I could enforce conduct, but whatever it's going to be I can't think too long. I have only instinct.

"No." Compassion wins.

The three of them look at me, then each other for a moment and then break into the same welcoming smile.

Francis holds his hands open on his lap and says quickly, "Sorry, sorry, sorry. We have to have our avenues for vetting candidates. So sorry if this caused you undue stress. And I know it did." He points to the wall behind me. A screen shows an abstract pink and blue image of my body—most vivid around the jeans, the shirt, and the boots. The colors throb with reddish pulses radiating out from my center. I watch for my inhalation, but it's not there. My passing confusion at this shows up, though, as a quick gray bubble through the pale shape of my head. My recognition that some kind of sensors in the clothes display the workings of my mind on the wall forms as a distinct yellow blob. The undulating red tinge on the edges, I assume, is paranoia. As soon as I conceive of *that*, the vibrating becomes more extreme and the red deepens. I try to visualize a placid field of sunflowers to soothe the palette, but I can't help wondering what else they've impregnated my clothing with, and the blob only becomes more frenetic. I can't hide here. They know exactly what they're getting.

Karuna gives me a friendly jab in the ribs. "I knew you couldn't turn me in."

At first, I am relieved that I passed. I look back at my body map and see, in soft blues, the shape of my emotions, calmed by my thoughts. Then I experience a moment's fury at being so watched. I don't want them to see it projected on the wall. By staring at my shape, I think I can figure out how to maintain the calm colors. Karuna comes over and gives me another jab. The man gives me a wink. These are my colleagues now. I'm part of a whole. The blue spreads down through my systems.

I laugh, pretending that I'm in with them on the joke. "Watching the blue feels good." Even saying so creates a loop and makes my whole body bluer.

They all look amused. I feel like I'm four years old.

I address Jeannie: "I'm not in a rush but I came here so prepared that I have to ask: When do you think we can sit down and really talk about my proposal?"

"Whoo boy," she says, with a snort, "you still don't understand what you've joined up for, do you?"

Best Medicine

I leave them badgering the nurse in the cafeteria. All I want is to appreciate the volcano alone, without the whole needy-crowd thing.

My niche is the last-hurrah set, folks with at least two major cancers or a primary ailment, but still sporty enough to manage a little adventure. I enjoy working with this segment, a hell of a lot more than being a salaried embezzler for the state. This crowd is fun, up for anything. Usually in their final stages before the real rattle begins, they're all terminal so they don't have a lot of hang-ups. No protective gear when they go in the sun, they drink water right from the faucet.

My biggest, most worthwhile expense is the nurse who comes along, making sure they're dosed with their proper medicines, hydrated and pumped full of enough steroids so they can stay vertical, climb the steps, brave the rapids. Thanks to her they just walk around free, hungry for everything, like last-minute shoppers trying to take home the whole store. Each one a little star, burning out brightly. The whole thing is kind of Zen, if you buy into that.

What I'm trying to wrap my mind around is why this particular group has been giving me trouble. I've got my little cancers too, I'm managing my own care regimen, so I have a decent idea of what they're going through. It's what makes me a good guide. Still, this crowd second-guesses me more as each day passes. Just now, when I came out here, the Unmarried Talker, whose powers of social insinuation have up till now been appreciated, grabs me at the elbow—so tenderly, as if I'm the weak one—to ask if maybe the group shouldn't skip the two-rope rappel down the cliff after lunch. *It's on the itinerary you all signed up for. Yes, you're all well enough to do it.*

At least the valley here has the tropical terrain they want. After the floods, the government went overboard trying to make the place look temperate, despite the new climate. They reintroduced all these native oaks, but the warm wind from the ocean blew them back into crazy angles toward the volcano, like they're praying to it. Finally, the landscape team gave in and started planting palms. For all the planning, what they forgot to add is some human-scale structure that could show you how big the volcano really is. Give the scene a little more wow.

Three times a year, I stand on this promenade and point to the iconic volcano, point to the fierce waves pounding into its base. "This," I tell my faux-interested charges, "is called a destructive plate margin."

They ask, "How long since the last eruption?"

"Thirty-two years." Then I give my joking smile. "You're safe."

That's when they each quietly wish they'd splurged for the extra day trip to see a live one in Japan. No matter what, you want an explosion, especially when you're going to die. This wimp here releases all of its pressure in dainty, white wisps.

Still, it serves as an engaging subject for contemplation and relaxation. An off-center pile of rocks, with that slinky volcanic curve up to kiss the sky. An innocent symbol of destruction, like the sun. My doctor encourages me to meditate on the natural world. *Get lost in it and find yourself,* like she's selling me a three-week safari. I humor her every now and then by trying one of these exercises because she also prescribes the serious bone-curdling meds when I need them.

So I study the hill, let it tell me the earth is round, filled with elaborate, molten plumbing. All this will allegedly lead to inner reliance and, eventually, clean detachment from the body—just what the doctor ordered. I close my eyes and project myself into the pale puffs, *to heal each of my cells with love.* Just for her.

I attempt to erase the two weeks I've been jetting these desperates around and the two weeks we've got before our last night of big fun, before they all scatter to their various and exclusive hospital towns to die. Why do I bother? Their cliques have been established, the subtle competitions are in place, their impressions of my skills are set. It's not like I'm banking on repeat business. For all practical purposes, I

186

could deliver them home tomorrow. But the money I'm taking is criminal. So we've got the mountain adventure, the rafting adventure, and the ski adventure to look forward to. Yee and hah.

I open my eyes. The volcano is still there, telling me nothing. My moment of contemplation was a washout. I've only succeeded in creating more cancerous adrenaline. I could sleep for a week.

Someone's there, on the edge of the crater, amid the clouds of hydrogen sulfide. It looks like a man dancing. He's got no details, he's practically made of smoke. The clouds blow in front and in back of this unlikely guy doing his jig, like an ant, as if the mountain just rose up under him. Now *he* gives you some sense of the scale.

I should visit my father.

Standing feels provisional. I spread my feet slightly for support, like you would on the back of a whale.

"That volcano is all right."

It's the Pregnant Teen, carrying some health drink in a giant bottle. She's suddenly next to me, terrorizing my space with an unsolicited pat on the shoulder. Wherever we go, she can be relied upon to alternate this kind of breathtaking insight with, "Would you look at that?"

She points the bottle at the volcano and says, "I see something like that and, I gotta say, I know exactly how it feels. You know where I'm coming from, don't you?" She's due in two months. They think the baby will make it.

I'm tempted to bestow a courtesy smile but, weighing that kindness against the prospect of being her only friend for the rest of the trip, I say, "Would you mind staying with the group?" She goes back inside, undoubtedly with a report to all that I'm moody. Fine, they can keep their distance.

I look back and the wind's changed; the steam is blowing in the other direction. The man on the crater is now exposed, a pile of rocks.

Still, I'm resolved about seeing Dad. It will dovetail nicely. In the last few days there's been a flurry of requests to squeeze an alternative healer onto the schedule. I'm sure Dad can play the part. We'll dump the cliff walk, which they've been complaining about anyway, and fly out this afternoon. We'll see him in the morning, then fly from there to base camp for the hike. The group will provide maximum distraction, and he can preach to them whatever he feels like preaching. The old freak will adore the attention.

No one seems sorry to miss the cliff walk, but I'm sure a comment will drift back to me at the end of the trip anyway. Some of them perk up when I promise a real-live shaman tomorrow. The prospect of getting on the plane to do so sinks them all into doubt. *Can't we find another healer nearby, today?* Fortunately, the nurse convinces them the treated air will be good for all of us even as she coaxes them up the stairs and into the jet.

Now they're settled and we're flying into a cloud, which even after all the flights I've taken still feels enchanted to me, like whatever happens in here isn't real.

Once we're cruising, I make the call from the back of the plane.

"Dad?"

"Who calls me Dad?" That old smile's in his voice.

"Only one person I know of."

"I wanted you to call me."

"And here I am."

"I mean I willed you to call me." So much for sane. I lean against the emergency door and see if anyone's paying attention. The nurse is forcing cups of antiviral water on everyone. I'm freezing all of a sudden and I motion for her to turn up the air. Down the aisle, the group is all plugged in to their viewers, watching trade data come in from all over the waking planet. I lower my voice, as if it will do any good. I'm sure at least one of them has a monitor on.

"I'm still doing tours, Dad."

"That's a surprise."

The plane bumps twice and we drop out of a cloud. All is visible again.

"I'm seeing so much, meeting all kinds of people. Every day I'm traveling. I work with the dying, Dad. I'm helping people."

"No explanation needed. Just glad to hear your voice. My surprise is only conceptual, that there are still tours, still sites to see. Still people to pay. But someone always has the money, right? You worked that out a long time ago, didn't you?"

"Are you still practicing?"

"I've stopped practicing and started doing. You're forty,

189

when are you going to learn from my mistakes?" He gives a cluck of that know-it-all laugh of his. "You're coming by?"

"Depends on you."

"A child's presence is a perpetual blessing."

"I think the group would like to have an audience."

"I'm not here for entertainment. And I'm not taking anyone's money if I can't help them."

"That's great, Dad."

"Are they chemically medicated?"

"They have their regimes, sure, but, come on, they're cornered; they're plenty curious about natural approaches."

I can hear him struggling to find an open mind about this. "If it means seeing my son, I'll meet these drugged little barons. When?"

"I'm actually calling from the plane."

He laughs. "I was ready before the phone even rang."

"Perfect."

I close the phone and look at them. From the back of the plane, I deliver the good news, "We're going to see a shaman."

There is some immediate grumbling, as I should have expected, but I walk through the plane to give directions to the pilot. It will be good to see him again. Sometime before the Barricades started, Dad quit, got us reclassified so we could live outside the city, bought ten acres in the mountains and started building his outpost, with safe water, safe air and a monumentally secure garden. A kind of paradise, really. My mother couldn't take it, but they let me decide for myself. I stayed with him for my fifteenth year, but I got bored easily back then and headed back to the city. At the time he said he understood my decision, that we each make the journeys we have to make, but every time we talk, he brings up things that happened during that year like we had a decade's worth of memories in it.

The nurse stops me first, no doubt to ask if I've taken my meds and to relay some new complaint from the group. As much as I appreciate her work, I don't cherish her coming at me like a union organizer every time I'm near. I accept her cup of water and squeeze past before she can even start. I notice a lump on her neck that might be new. I don't want to bring up anything that might slow us down.

The Unmarried Talker comes over to my seat behind the pilot and relates that she once produced an entertainment segment on *fabricated shamans*—generally middle-aged white guys who pay someone for a vision quest and get themselves ordained without authentic experience. I look behind her and see she's already shared this nugget with everyone else on the plane. She leans in close with her toxic breath and says, "Honestly, no one worth their salt calls themselves a shaman anymore. Even the few indigenous tribes left have let it go. Maybe we could visit one of those plant labs, where they're really advancing *effective* therapies?"

I clear my throat and cough a little to show I know they're all against me. It turns into a hack, which after ten seconds really gets their attention. The nurse comes at me with her syrup. I keep her back. "OK, I used *shaman* as shorthand. He doesn't call himself that so much. The land there is majestic and sublime at the same time. You'll see another kind of lifestyle. You'll all be enlightened, don't worry." I cough again, emphasizing finality, but again it continues till I'm wheezing. The Talker backs off, throwing her hands up at the others. I realize I'm drenched in sweat. Lately flying has been giving me a flush. The nurse quietly hands me a towel to dry my face. Super.

Dad used *shaman* only once to me. When I started making meaningful money, I was able visit more often. He was already well on his way—the hair, the fingernails, feral. He lived off the land and practiced whatever he practiced on the locals for barter. I was having my first cancer then. He tried to take my meds away, swore he owed his health to renouncing devil pharmaceuticals. He looked well enough. He hadn't died out there after all, he'd gotten through five treatments before he was fifty. He was sorry he'd ever let me go back to the city and all the trouble I made. I tried to take him to the city, take him shopping. He wouldn't have it, wouldn't even let me leave any money. Said he wouldn't know what to do with it. He promised he would one day heal me for good.

I should have told them he was a wizard, which, by his reckoning, he probably is by now. I don't care. Even if he's only ranting, he'll be something to see, and probably appreciate the attention of a son who seems to be honoring his delusions.

The Shaky Widow asks if the detour is going to cost extra because she knows of a superior clinic right near the base camp we're going to tomorrow. She struggles to pose this as a general accounting concern when it's so nakedly a matter of her not quite being able to swing this trip in the first place.

She's clearly got some sort of bet going as to which is going to give out first, her health or her money. Let's hope it's neither for now. I'm not remotely interested in organizing an airlift from the mountain.

"No extra cost," I assure her. "I'll spring for this flight."

When I finally talk to the pilot, the nurse tells the muttering throng, disobeying every bit of protocol, "The man is his father. We should just go." She's probably been monitoring me this whole trip. I'm not talking to her, I'm not hiring her again.

Machiavelli leans out of the aisle to tell me, "I don't care if he is your father, if he's the genuine article, he won't agree to see us en masse."

The Miserable Couple says, almost in unison, "And certainly not at the hotel."

Machiavelli adds, "We're already up, why not keep flying and visit one of the hospitals just over the border? They're doing some amazing work."

Everyone loves this idea. I raise my open hands.

"Because this isn't a medical tour. We've all seen enough clinics. You've had enough experiments. I'm trying to expose us to something a little different. OK. Tonight we'll have a hearty meal. I think we could all use a little meat—steak anyone? My treat! Then, before bed, let's get you all into the pool. Hog the spa jets, they'll do you good. In the morning—my gift to you—we'll go see him. At minimum, he'll give us a blessing for our trip. At most, what? You're all cured." This breaks it open, everyone has a nice nervous chuckle.

Having already done her damage, the nurse works the

crowd. "Maybe we have the time, maybe the man is a healer of some sort, and since he hasn't seen his son in a while, it could be important."

They seem to listen to her but I don't want it to be too much about me so I seal it right there. "Remember: We all need to get a good night's sleep. You're putting packs on those backs tomorrow afternoon."

On the bus in the morning, I sit next to Anthony, who is enjoying the rare privilege of taking a second tour with me. Some experimental drug cured his cancer but muted half his vision and hearing. His trick is to feel his way to the best vantage point of a site—the edge of a waterfall, the bottom of a canyon—and announce, "Hey, at least I'm standing." Like that's the meaning of life.

It's not till we're cruising around a curve that I realize he's resting his hand on mine. We're both blistered, raw and, apparently, insensate from our respective prescriptions. For a moment, I can't tell which scarred bit of flesh is mine. This sucks. I look like the rest of them. I disengage our skin. I get out my coverup cream to smooth down the dark orange patches. Dad's going to have some words to say about this. I'll get lectures about purity of treatment. Undoubtedly, he'll reach for something he's ground together from the back of the garden. Or maybe it's simpler now. All he'll do is touch me and I'll be made well.

The bus turns left at the mailbox post, which hasn't

changed since Dad bought the land. We climb up the gravel road with steady power. The path is decorated with all sorts of tribal hoo-hahs. Sticks tied to rocks (with braids of silver hair from my father's ridiculous mane, no doubt) and stuck in the ground to ward off evil, welcome friends, whatever he's in the mood for. Vaguely sinister. This whole group has been living the medical life so long that even this glimpse of solitary living must be a treat.

We get up to the driveway and the house is gone. A two-story maroon cottage, with a tile roof, black shutters, gone. The original beams still stand in a Stonehenge silence with all sorts of colored fabric pinned to frame the space where it once stood. Flags for his fort, hanging there with no breeze. Three army tents are set up on dark blue tarp, where the front lawn was. Dad runs out from one of them, authoritatively directing the coach into the only unplanted space on the property. We pull onto a pebbled driveway where the garage used to be.

Dad's not wearing anything protective. In fact, he's only wearing what looks like a batik diaper. His hair and eyebrows are gone. But his skin is clear and his body is muscled, his eyes still healthy and gleaming, so it's not from medicine. There's a cut on the side of his head, a thin line of blood over one ear. What a host. He shaved off all his hair for us. Excellent: The group will get their live freak show and I'll get points for visiting.

Dad shoves his grinning face next to the window, trying to see through the mirrored glass. All bald men look like chimps, and he's no exception. He walks up to the front, taps on the door and I unlock the seal. The air that escapes seems to knock him back. He covers his face with his arm.

"What are you people breathing in there?"

The Young Man of Independent Means, who sits in the front any chance he gets, tells him, "It's pumped for immunity."

I wish that hadn't been the opening salvo. Dad regains enough composure to come back at us with a tense smile, continuing to fan the air.

"Come outside and get a breath of what we've got here." He inhales deeply and his eyes roll to white. The air is apparently so magnificent that he loses words and holds his arms out to the heavens. It's that good. He stands with his hands in prayer position, awaiting our collective rush to hug him.

Anthony tilts his head like a bird at the others. "What are you all waiting on?" He heaves up, steadies himself on the seat backs and pulls his way through the aisle. His fingers turn nearly purple as he clutches the railing going down. Waiting at the bottom step, Dad catches him in his arms like a child.

The others turn to me with concern. I don't move, not yet.

"Don't you want to say hello?" the Pregnant Teen asks, dabbing my face with a napkin. Suddenly I realize how kind she's been to me this whole trip and I feel my guts drop, like everything is going to fall out of me.

"Not yet. Go ahead," I say, ushering everyone off. Steadying myself on the arm rails, I watch him greet them all, rubbing them in the right places, making them comfortable,

196

learning their names. They're all breathing it in as deeply as they can. The still, natural air, the smell of his skin. When was the last time any of these people were touched like this? Soon the scene becomes one enormous love-in, the whole group reaching around and gently feeling each other's bodies. I watch from the top steps of the bus, proud. No, they won't complain about this stop. And Dad looks happy. He turns to the bus.

"I think there's one more in there!"

I'm stuck on the second step. Before I can come down, he leaps in and surrounds me.

"I'm sick too, Dad."

"I know," he says, supporting my head. "We'll get you fixed up. Come outside."

"I don't know if I can."

He yells out, "We need some help here."

Suddenly I'm being carried down the steps of the bus, supported at my shoulders and my knees. Outside, I look up into my father's eyes. You've never seen a color like this, like a bucket of summer peas. I relax into it, like my doctor told me to. For a moment, I feel that space she's always talking about, like I'm holding on to this world by a string. I hold it and let it go, hold it and let it go. When I let it go, when I close my eyes, I drift, but when I open them he's looking at me with the sun behind him and I'm holding on.

Everyone supports a different limb so the skin won't tear. We all learn so much about treatment from each other. They carry me across the land that used to be our house and place me on the tarp. A twig underneath pokes my shoulder. I try to shift from it, but can't. I can't tell them, can't talk. I feel like I've been fighting for so long. They're standing all around now, looking nervous, except for Dad. He kneels down next to me, kisses my forehead in three places, tells me I'm going to be all right.

The nurse says, "He was doing poorly, but then his medication seemed to have stopped working altogether in the last forty-eight."

All I know is I'm looking up into this green that's looking back at me, this green that I've heard about my whole life because I have it too. People meet me and have to comment on it—as if I didn't know the color of my own eyes. I always think, *You ought to meet my father.*

He looks to the sky as he feels the pulse on my neck, on my wrists, on my feet. I count too, like he taught me, trying to feel the pulse in his fingers, watching his breath.

He rubs his healing hands together, then lays them on my scalp, my forehead, my chin.

The nurse says, "I knew it. It's too late." Such a worrier. She can take the group back home. I'm staying here.

Someone says, "Shhh! Let him work."

My father is undressing me, examining my body, this map of my failures. He sees my lips move. I taste the salt on my skin. I must be dehydrated. I attempt to tell him, but I'm not sure what comes out.

"I need your help," my father says to the others, "but I also need space." The group obediently widens the circle around us. He urges two of them, I can't see who, to lay their hands on my feet, as if they're holding me in place. He positions himself at my other end, cradling my head on his knees.

He rubs his hands together again and then separates them over my face. I'm looking at the lines on his palms. Poor man. He's been working hard. I suddenly realize that it's better here with him than anywhere I've been. I want to apologize for my fifteenth year. I'm ready to live like this. I want to tell him that I'm going to stay and take care of him.

He inhales deeply, summoning his powers. His hands come slowly down, working from my forehead to my chin and back again, pressing a current of air tight between us. I see it rushing across my face. Slowly, he lowers his fingertips nearer my skin till I can feel their heat on my cheeks and then, without a sound, without the slightest incantation, he closes my eyes.